HOW TO ROB A TRAIN

HOW TO ROB A TRAIN

The Man Behind Britain's
Most Notorious Robbery,
Among Other Things

GORDON GOODY
with
Maurice O'Connor

Milo Books Ltd

Published in November 2014 by Milo Books

ISBN 978-1-908479-81-5

Typeset by Jayne Walsh

Printed in Great Britain by Cox and Wyman, Reading, Berkshire

MILO BOOKS LTD

www.milobooks.com

'Steal a little, you're a thief
Steal a lot, you're a king.'

Anon.

Contents

Introduction

I CAN SCARCELY believe it is more than fifty years ago that I and a set of pals set out on a bit of work that would become the most infamous robbery in British criminal history. The Glasgow to London mail train hurtling along the tracks in the early hours of 8 August 1963 was carrying £2.6 million – nearly £50 million in today's money – and we were about to go out and steal it.

There are certain historical events so memorable that anyone who was around at the time can remember vividly where they were and what they were doing when the news broke. The assassination of John F. Kennedy, Princess Diana's death and the destruction of the Twin Towers are the prime examples in my lifetime. Although of much less consequence, an awful lot of people who were around on that summer day will remember the news breaking of the Great Train Robbery.

The resulting investigations would lead to the longest trial, the longest jury deliberations and the longest sentences for robbery in British legal history. This is the story of my part in it and I think it's fair to say that without me there wouldn't have been a Great Train Robbery. Then again, without the Ulsterman acquiring the information and without him passing it to Brian Field, who made the introduction to me, there wouldn't have been a robbery either. So let's just call it a team effort.

Despite all that's been said, written and even filmed about the robbery, many of the details have never seen the light of day. Many of the things published as fact were total fantasy. Perhaps it's time for the myths to be exploded and the true story to be told before I go.

Let me make one thing perfectly clear from the start. Bruce Reynolds has been a very close personal friend of mine for most of our lives and remained so until his death in February 2013, but I do take exception to being referred to, as I have been from time to time, as Bruce's number two. I wasn't number two to anybody. Whilst admittedly there were some of us more number one than others, there was never a single number one. Most decisions were arrived at by consensus and very rarely were there any disagreements.

It didn't take me long after meeting Bruce to realise that he and I were like chalk and cheese, but that's not such a bad thing when planning a caper: being able to look at things from different perspectives. Bruce freely admitted that he craved 'peer recognition'. If he couldn't be the best thief in London he certainly wanted to be one of the best. He liked to cast himself in the role of a Raffles-type gentleman burglar and he wanted to be able to walk into a pub and have people mutter, 'That's Bruce Reynolds, the master criminal.'

There was nothing I craved less than peer recognition or any other sort of recognition come to that. I wanted nothing more than the money, plain and simple.

Bruce loved the bright lights and the pubs and clubs of Soho, the wining and dining and socialising, the flash cars and the expensive clothes.

I did most of these things myself but not to the same extent as Bruce. I was much more content in a country pub and following pursuits like fishing and hunting.

One thing we were in total accord with was violence, or rather the absence of it. You can't be in the robbery business without accepting that there will be times when violence cannot be avoided but we were determined to keep it to the absolute minimum and only as a last resort. This wasn't just for humanitarian reasons. Sentences for robbery were often directly proportional to the amount of violence employed so why compound the offence if the objective could be achieved with a little subtlety?

Another area of common ground we had was the time and effort we put into planning and precautions like alibis and disguises. If you can prove fairly categorically that you were in a certain place at a certain time then obviously you couldn't have been getting up to whatever the law claimed you'd been getting up to.

Because of my physique – six foot three and well built – disguise was a bit more important to me than it was to more averagely built people. Over the years I became adept in the use of wigs, hair dye, false moustaches and beards, make-up and masks. I had one India-rubber mask that was so lifelike that when I took it off after a bit of work a colleague begged me to replace it saying I looked better with it on.

Gordon Goody
Vera, Almeria, Spain

1

Army and Navy

IT IS hard to imagine from my humble beginnings that I would go on to lead the adventurous life that I have: safe-blowing, armoured car robbery and, of course, the odd train robbery.

It all started in Northern Ireland. Although I was born in Oxford in 1930, I was shipped off to Cookstown, County Tyrone, Northern Ireland, at just a few days old. My mother was in domestic service and my father was a soldier and it was thought best that I was reared by my aunt and uncle, so off I went.

It was a very rural life. My guardians had little money but we never went short of much. My uncle worked as a chicken breeder and at a very early age I went into the business myself. A pal's father owned a small, abandoned farmstead and we fenced off a field and set about stealing the odd chicken here and there. The wholesaler who dealt with my uncle was only too happy to take them off our hands, in the strictest of confidence of course.

Schooling came very low on my list of priorities, the kids being expected to contribute to the farm work almost from the time they could walk. I did briefly attend Glenarny's National Boys' School, to which I travelled every day on a donkey. I used to tether it across the way in Glasgow's Field but one day it was stolen and I never saw it again.

I hated the school with a passion, not least of all because my form master, Baldy McCullough, was an unmitigated sadistic bully. His idea of chastisement was to send the current 'best boy', generally a little shit called Samuel, out with a penknife to cut a sally-rod from the hedgerow. Baldy would then spend a few minutes trimming it up, with all the class waiting in trepidation to see who his latest victim would be. There was none of that nonsense about holding out your hand or even bending over. Baldy would simply lash out at any exposed part of the unfortunate's body: head, back, legs, arms or anywhere else.

Couldn't happen these days. Baldy would no doubt be nicked, charged with GBH and get himself a five stretch. I'm the last person in the world to want to see anyone getting nicked but if anyone deserved a bit of bird it was Baldy.

Schooling apart, I did love the rural life though and to this day I'm a country boy at heart. I've always kept dogs and my hobbies were the usual country pursuits of hunting, shooting and fishing.

One Sunday afternoon I was out hunting rabbits with my dog and when he disappeared into a hedgerow I gave chase. I came across what seemed to be a metal box with the back ripped off and, rummaging through some old papers inside, I discovered a half-crown. This was a fortune to a young lad seventy-odd years ago and much too big a piece of good luck to keep to myself. I told all my pals.

Before long someone, probably that little shit Samuel again, grassed me up to Baldy. My dishonesty in keeping the half-crown was sufficient justification in Baldy's eyes to dispatch the 'best boy' out with the penknife. Baldy then went through the usual procedure of lashing every accessible part of my anatomy.

As luck would have it that day my father had come home unexpectedly on leave and was waiting to surprise me at the school gates. When he saw the state of me and heard what had happened he decided to wait for Baldy and have a word with him. Next thing the bully was sprawled across the bonnet of his car with my dad's hands around his throat. I didn't hear the full content of the conversation but the gist of it was that if he ever laid a finger on me again Dad would be back for a more serious chat. Shortly afterwards I was elevated to the lofty heights of 'best boy'. In common with most bullies Baldy was also a coward.

Baldy took me in his car to the local nick and I had to show the bobby where I'd found the box. This would be the first of a lifetime series of run-ins with the Old Bill. It turned out the box was a safe that had been taken out of a cinema in a nearby town and the police took it away for examination. No further mention was made of the half-crown but I did learn a valuable lesson from the whole escapade. When you have a little tickle don't breathe a word to a soul.

My uncle graduated from chicken farming to cattle farming. At the time there was some sort of incentive scheme whereby the carcasses of cattle reared in the North were worth £2 or £3 a hundredweight more than cattle reared in the South. At the customs post, imported cattle had a hole clipped in their ears to distinguish them from their Northern cousins.

My uncle would buy a small herd and load them on his truck. A couple of hundred yards from the border we'd stop and unload them. I'd drive them through a gate, across a field and out through another gate. We were now in the North with the cattle's ears intact. On a herd of ten or twelve, weighing five or six hundredweight each, this was a colossal earner and my uncle did very well out of it.

IN 1942, I RETURNED to London, where my parents had a flat in Queen's Gate, and was enrolled, again briefly, at Oakham Road School. There was no bullying there but I still had no great enthusiasm for schooling.

It wasn't a great time to be living in central London. Although the Blitz had finished the previous autumn there were still isolated bombing raids over the docks and the East End.

I was taking the dog for a walk in Kensington Gardens one afternoon when he suddenly planted himself and refused to budge. After a fruitless minute or two of tugging at the lead I heard the sound of the air-raid sirens. Dogs have much more acute hearing than humans and he obviously heard the sirens before I did and that was what was frightening him.

As I turned to seek shelter in South Ken tube station there was a tremendous explosion about a hundred yards up the street. A group of five American GIs who had been standing on the corner were blown to smithereens. Had the dog not planted himself that was about the point I would have reached before hearing the sirens. I learned later that the explosion wasn't a bomb but an anti-aircraft projectile that had failed to explode in mid-air as they're designed to do. Instead it had exploded in the midst of the GIs. I suppose nowadays they'd refer to that as friendly fire but it didn't appear too friendly to me at the time.

The most spectacular blaze occurred when flying bombs struck Price's candle factory over in Battersea. It was weeks before the fire was brought under control.

That was far from the only devastation I witnessed. One night there was the usual pandemonium of guns blazing and searchlights sweeping the sky. Two bombs exploded at the junction of Putney Bridge Road and Putney High Street. It's hard to think of a busier intersection, what with the Milk Bar and the Glass Slipper dancehall above and three cinemas, the Palace, the Regal and the Hippodrome, all within a matter of yards. It was total carnage with a total of eighty-one people killed and God knows how many injured. My father was a local man who was born in the windmill on Wimbledon Common where his father, my grandfather, was a common ranger. He went to help recover the bodies and take them to the Palace, which had the seats ripped out and was used as a temporary mortuary. By coincidence I was in the same refurbished Palace cinema on 15 August 1945 watching the Billy Wilder film *Five Graves To Cairo* when, midway through, the house lights were turned up and the manager came on stage to announce that the Japanese had surrendered and the war was finally over. By way of celebration the manager produced a bunch of bananas, fruit being in very short supply at that time, and auctioned them off.

Ironically enough for one of my old stomping grounds, the site of the Palace cinema would later become the Criminal Records Office.

I had another near-death experience around that time. I was working as a paperboy and on my round was a large, detached residence called Manor Fields. There was a dog yapping in a greenhouse and I wandered around to investigate. Mooching about I discovered a .22 BSA rifle and a box of cartridges, which I snaffled.

A week later I was going for a trip back to Northern Ireland and decided to take the rifle with me since there would be more opportunity for hunting expeditions. There was very little in the way of customs control between Ulster and the mainland so I just stuck it in my suitcase.

My pal Tommy Hamilton and I travelled over on the ferry *Princess Maude* from Stranraer to Larne. This was the first time I ever experienced hot water coming from a tap; I thought hot water only came out of a kettle. That's progress for you. Incidentally, the *Princess Maude* was the last boat to leave the beaches at Dunkirk during the evacuation of the British Expeditionary Force.

At the weekend Tommy and I went out to do a spot of hunting and by mid-afternoon we were taking a break, lying on the grass verge. Around the corner came a vehicle known as a Crossley, a sort of armoured personnel carrier used by the Royal Ulster Constabulary. Not having bothered with formalities like a gun licence, I thought it best to put the rifle out of sight. As I slid it behind me under a bush, a twig must have caught on the trigger, causing the rifle to fire. The bullet missed my head by something like a millimetre. The Old Bill stopped to investigate, found the rifle and confiscated it but no charges ensued.

Back in London I decided I'd had enough of school and paper rounds and that it was time to get a proper job. My father was insistent that I learn a trade and he got me a job as a plumber's mate. The company was called Rawling Brothers and some years later they would devise and patent the now world-famous Rawl Plug.

Amongst other activities this company had a locksmith department. Years later I went back and burgled the place, taking everything I could carry by way of locks, key-blanks, files and tools. I spent hour upon hour dismantling and re-assembling the locks. By removing the backs and inserting a sheet of plastic I could see how the tumblers and pins worked and I became something of an expert on them. I also became a fairly adept key maker. All this would come in very handy in my future career.

MY FIRST MAJOR run-in with the Old Bill came on 2 March 1948, when I was seventeen, and it's not something I take any pride in. A pal and I were in an amusement arcade just lounging about when we got into conversation with a middle-aged bloke. Before long he was making sexual advances to my pal. We left the arcade and the bloke followed us, continuing behind as we entered an alleyway. To cut a long story short, we gave him a few slaps and relieved him of his wallet. As I say, not something I'm proud of.

I was arrested shortly afterwards and the man identified me. I was charged with robbery with violence and on conviction at the Central Criminal Court (the Old Bailey) was sentenced to twenty-one months and twelve strokes of the birch. It's hard to believe that as recently as the fifties the use of something as medieval as corporal punishment was still common in Britain. In fact, while it was done away with as a judicial sentence in the fifties it was still available as a punishment for breaches of prison discipline until 1967. It's also quite hard to explain how painful birching is to someone who has never experienced it.

I was sent to the notorious Wormwood Scrubs Prison in west London to serve my sentence and it was there that the birching was administered. The birch is a bundle of four or five narrow birch branches plaited together, weighing some sixteen ounces and around four feet long. The prisoner is tied to a wooden A-frame with his hands above his head, stripped to the waist. The strokes are administered to the back and shoulders and, since there would be no point employing a wimp, the screw doing the lashing tended to be one of those big, strapping chaps. As some slight concession to fair play the screw is not allowed to bend his arm when administering the strokes. The first few lashes are painful enough but the real agony comes towards the end as the strokes begin to overlap, causing welts and breaking of the skin.

I suppose the whole thing didn't last more than a couple of minutes but it seemed like an eternity and my back was a raw, bloody mess. When it was over I couldn't walk. I was surrounded by about a dozen people – governor, assistant governor, a few screws of various rank, a doctor and some bloke from the Home Office – so it wasn't just painful, it was fucking embarrassing. I was attended to by the doctor on a daily basis for the first two weeks, my blood blisters were squeezed and burst and a balm was applied. I'm a big strapping chap myself but it took me weeks to get over the experience.

I mention this episode not so much to curry sympathy as to illustrate how harsh the British penal system was back in the fifties and sixties. And it wasn't just the brutality. The workshops were silent and the work itself the most tedious imaginable, sewing mailbags being the normal employment for the bulk of the inmates. If you watch crime films from that period you usually see the 'ex-con' talking out of the corner of his mouth. Talking anywhere except for the hour on the exercise yard was prohibited and even there you were only allowed to talk to the person immediately alongside you. If you wanted a furtive conversation with someone in front or behind the only option was to whisper out of the side of the mouth in a way that wasn't visible to the prevailing screw. Diet gave no relief to the tedium either as the basic ingredients for the three daily meals were porridge (actually labelled 'number 3 pig meal'), potatoes and bread. Altogether a much more draconian regime than prevails these days (or so I've been led to believe).

I was released in 1949 but it wasn't long before I was back before the beak. My second conviction in 1950 was a total fit-up and I was completely innocent. Later in this book I will mention several other incidents where I claim to have been fitted up and a sceptic my well say, 'Oh, come on. Once, okay. Twice, maybe. But any more than that I'm not having.'

This might be a good time for me to try and illustrate the climate back then. Your average, law-abiding citizen came into little or no contact with the Old Bill, other than maybe to ask the time or for directions. There were few cars about so even speeding and parking tickets rarely came into play. Joe Public assumed all police officers were cast in the mould of Dixon of Dock Green and to try to convince him that a policeman was telling lies was like trying to plait fog.

There was, probably still is, a rule that said that a defendant's previous convictions couldn't be disclosed to the jury. The verdict had to be decided on the basis of the evidence in the charge before them. Very nice to have the odd rule in your favour. However, if a defendant challenged the integrity of a witness, that rule went out of the window. If a defendant had form, the worst thing he could possibly do was accuse a policeman of lying.

A cross-examination could often go along these lines:

'Mr Smith, Detective Sergeant Bloggs has testified that when he arrested you, you said, "It's a fair cop, guv. I'll hold my hands up." Is that correct?'

'No.'

'NO? Are you suggesting the officer is lying?'

'Certainly not. I think he's mistaken.'

'MISTAKEN? The officer wrote it down in his diary. How can he be mistaken?'

'I don't know, sir. All I'm saying is I didn't say that.'

This rigmarole can go backwards and forwards for an inordinate length of time but should Mr Smith lose his temper and say something like 'Oh, bollocks. Yes, I'm saying he's lying, the same as the fat slag lied every other time he's given evidence against me,' well now Mr Smith has well and truly pissed on his chips. His form will be read out and, just to be fair to everyone, the police officer's record, with his fifteen years of impeccable service, half dozen commendations for bravery and the amount of his spare time he devotes to under-privileged kids will also be read out. There's not the slightest chance on this planet of Mr Smith getting a not guilty.

As recently as the late seventies there was a law in London, possibly nationwide, known as the Sus Law. This was the informal name for the stop-and-search law, which allowed police officers to stop, search and potentially arrest suspects on suspicion of having done something. A very common charge was 'attempted theft from persons unknown'.

A plain-clothes policeman would testify that he was on a tube station platform and he saw the accused attempting to pick a pocket or steal a handbag. By the time he'd arrested the perpetrator, the intended victim had boarded a train and so was unidentifiable.

If you have form and therefore can't challenge the Old Bill version of events, how on earth are you going to get out of a charge like that? Well, you're not. The police justified all this, at least to themselves, by insisting they only targeted known thieves and pickpockets who, even if they hadn't done anything at that precise moment, had done something shortly before or were about to do something in the near future. That may well be true but there's no doubt innocent people were caught in the crossfire.

Police brutality was another issue, though I experienced little of this myself, being the size I was. Corporal punishment wasn't abolished in British prisons until 1967 so I suppose the Old Bill thought they had a licence to bash prisoners up. Police did frequently beat confessions out of people and it wasn't unheard of for an innocent person to break down and confess to something he hadn't done to avoid further punishment. Doesn't happen much these days what with recorded and video-taped interviews and all that. I had a pal who was nicked a few years back in London and at the nick the desk sergeant asked if he wanted anyone notified of his arrest.

'Yes,' he said, 'I want to be examined by a doctor to establish I have no cuts or bruises.'

'Fucking hell,' replied the sergeant, an oldish chap obviously with a fair number of years' experience. 'How long is it since you've been nicked? We don't beat people up any more.'

When you get into the realms of major crime, where top professional criminals come into conflict with expert criminal investigators, it has to be remembered that there is a very fine dividing line between them. At some point in their lives one mob decided to go one way while the other mob went the other. You must bear in mind that a policeman's prospects of promotion were directly proportional to his clear-up rate so if he was ambitious he had every incentive to embellish borderline cases.

People have no difficulty believing that a criminal will lie, cheat, threaten and bribe to get out of a charge. I've done so myself on numerous occasions. Why do they find it hard to believe that police will do exactly the same? It's perfectly routine procedure for police to offer a minor, and sometimes not so minor, crook leniency or even money to inform against colleagues. If a crucial piece of prosecution evidence has been excluded for some legal technicality, as sometimes happens, is it so hard to believe that the police will go to extremes to balance the scales? They know that had the evidence been allowed they would probably get a conviction so are fully prepared to embellish existing evidence or even fabricate a bit of new stuff. If the police know for a fact that a defence witness is lying through his or her teeth they'll have no compunction in getting one of their own to stand up and do the same. It was all part of the game we were playing

All this brings me back to my 1950 conviction. I had taken a girlfriend to the cinema and crossing Leicester Square we came across a street performer doing one of those escapology acts. We stood and watched and the next minute a detective appeared on each side of me. They claimed they'd seen me putting my hand in a man's pocket and arrested me for attempted theft. All I can tell you is that it didn't happen.

I was found guilty and at the time this made me in breach of a binding-over order for something so trivial I can't even remember what it was. The net result was I was gaoled for nine months.

AFTER RELEASE FROM prison, I was called up to do my National Service. They sent me for basic training to Bulford Camp on Salisbury Plain but I'd only been there a couple of weeks when I had a fallout with an NCO and wound up giving him a right hook. I spent the next few weeks on the trot back in London until my father grassed me up to the red-caps. He felt it was better for me to face the music with the army than to be hanging about penniless in London getting myself into even bigger trouble.

I was taken to Woolwich Arsenal and sentenced to twenty-one days 'parading with the guard', which was a fairly lenient sentence and had to be served back at Bulford. I had to turn out three times a day in full kit: rucksack, greatcoat, rifle, polished boots and blanco'd webbing.

At the evening parade on the twentieth night the sergeant-major, a decent chap called Hardacre, bellowed, 'Gunner Goody, have you read today's Part Eleven orders?'

Since reading Part 11 orders was one of the tasks I was obliged to do, lying through my teeth, I replied, 'Yes, sergeant major.'

'Gunner Goody, I'll ask you again. Have you read today's Part Eleven orders?'

'I have, sergeant major,' I lied again.

'Then I suggest you double over to the guardhouse and re-read them.'

Off I went at the double and began reading through them. Half way through I came to an item, 'Goody, Douglas Gordon, promoted to lance-bombardier'. They'd given me a stripe! Who dishes out these stripes, and quite why whoever it was considered I warranted one, remains a mystery to me to this day. Maybe Hardacre had seen something in me. However, it did have the effect of making me settle down to military life. I was posted to the Royal Artillery and I learned a fair amount about explosives, another attribute that would stand me in good stead in later life.

By the end of my National Service in 1952 I had risen to the rank of sergeant. The highlight of my time in the army was being part of an honour guard at St Paul's Cathedral in 1951. The occasion was entitled 'They Died for Independence' and was a memorial to the 28,000 American casualties killed whilst fighting with the Allies. It was attended by many dignitaries including the then Princess Elizabeth and Winston Churchill. The lesson was read by actor Douglas Fairbanks Jnr, who had risen to the rank of vice-admiral in the American navy during the war. *Time* magazine, or one of those other glossy monthlies, printed a front cover photo of the occasion and amongst GIs and sailors was a squad of British soldiers led by one Sgt Goody. I believe another participant in this parade was one Maurice Micklewhite. He later became more famous as the actor Michael Caine. I don't recall him but I've heard he mentions it in his own book.

I was asked to re-enlist and make the army my career, which I thought about but decided there were other things

I wanted to try. Not specifically robbing banks and blowing safes, though that's how things turned out. I did try a few straight jobs, one of which was selling those cardboard periscopes to the crowds standing on The Mall on the day of the Coronation, and a few other menial jobs.

My relationship with my father was strained, Dad being a bit of an authoritarian and myself being at a rebellious age. In 1953 we had a bad fight and I packed my bags and moved out. My mother would clandestinely meet me in parks and cinemas to give me some money, make sure I was getting enough to eat and all the other things a mother worries about. One Sunday morning I was waiting to meet her on Putney Bridge when a reporter came up to speak to me. He pointed across to a dock where the barges tied up and asked me if that was the spot where John Christie had been arrested that morning. Christie was Britain's first recognised serial killer and had murdered at least eight women, including his wife, Ethel. He had lived not far away at 10 Rillington Place, Notting Hill, and had given evidence three years earlier at the trial of his lodger, Timothy Evans, who was charged with the murders of his own wife and daughter, murders that in all probability Christie himself had committed. Evans was found guilty of the murder of his daughter and despite being slightly retarded was sentenced to death. He later received a posthumous pardon, while Christie was executed. Apparently I'd missed his arrest by a matter of hours.

Before long my mother arrived and while we sat chatting my father appeared on his bike. I thought we were going to have another row but I was wrong.

'Sit down son,' he said. 'Look, don't be so stupid. I want you to come home.'

Much as I wanted to go home too, I was very stubborn.

'I don't want to fucking come home,' I lied, trying to put a brave face on.

'Come home and we'll never talk about it again,' he said.

EVENTUALLY I LET HIM talk me into it. From that day on my relationship with my father was the closest it had ever been.

I thought I would give the Merchant Navy a go and in June 1953 I signed on with P&O as a cabin steward. My first voyage was to Australia, leaving on June 8 aboard the mv *Daffodil*. This was in the days of the £10 assisted passage and most of the passengers were impoverished unemployed seeking a new life in the colonies. So there was not much in the way of tips for a cabin steward but, had I been born a bit earlier in the days of transportation, I might well have been travelling to Australia under very different circumstances, shackled in the hold.

Arriving in Sidney, I decided to go and visit a pal, Dennis, who had done his National Service with me and was now a sergeant in the Australian army. I hadn't realised the vastness of the Outback and set off hitch-hiking to Dennis's camp miles out in the boonies. I got a lift in a wagon that defies description as regards size. There was the truck with three or four trailers attached, each loaded to the gunnels with sheep, probably three or four hundred of the things. The driver dropped me at the camp and Dennis and I went out for a drink, over which he tried to talk me into signing up and joining him. He reckoned with my fairly adequate National Service record I'd be a shoo-in to be enlisted with good prospects of promotion. I was tempted but at that point I'd had enough of army life and set off hitching back to Sidney. I arrived back at the harbour as they were about to raise the gang-plank and only got on board by the skin of my teeth. Had I arrived ten minutes later I'd have been stranded and probably been obliged to give Dennis's suggestion more thought. Maybe things would have worked out differently.

The voyage back was pretty uneventful barring one of the passengers dropping dead from a heart attack. He was an elderly Brit who'd made a lot of money in the sheep business and was returning to Britain to enjoy it, but it wasn't to be. He was buried at sea.

When we arrived back at Southampton I took some leave and then joined the mv *Orantes* on July 17 as a steward and assistant barman. This engagement lasted until October 6 and for the second time my seaman's book showed my character as 'good'. The seaman's book was a little perk for any registered merchant sailor and it could be used instead of a passport to gain entry to any port in the world.

I'd given the Merchant Navy my best shot but it was no more the life for me than the army had been. I suppose this was the time I decided that I was destined for a life of crime. I have often wondered since what made me go down this road, and there is no answer to it. I just wanted to be a burglar, it was as simple as that. I still had possession of my seaman's book which was a very comforting feeling. Should the need ever arise for a sudden clandestine departure from England, I wouldn't be faced with the expense and incon-venience of obtaining a black market passport.

2

A Life of Crime

MY FIRST SERIOUS piece of villainy was screwing Krantz Gents Outfitters on the Kings Road, Hammersmith. A pal and I cleaned the place out, not earning any fortunes but I thought a bit of bread and butter stuff would get me by until something bigger came along. A week or two later my pal was arrested and I thought I'd better make myself scarce in case my name came up as being an associate of his. I was sharing a flat with a girlfriend in Fulham who was herself on the run from her foster parents when one morning the door crashed open and in stormed two detectives. They dragged us both out of bed starkers and seemed more interested in ogling the naked young bird than arresting me, but eventually they told me to get dressed and accompany them to Hammersmith nick.

On the mantelpiece I had a comb-case containing six of what we used to call 'double-enders'. These were a type of skeleton key, a thin bar of steel with a filed-down key blank attached to either end. There weren't many locks that I couldn't open with one or another of these and I knew I'd have a problem if the Old Bill found them.

Fortunately enough the detectives were paying more attention to watching my girlfriend, who wasn't a bad sort, getting dressed than they were to me and I managed to slip the comb-case into my underpants. I did this more to stop the Old Bill finding them than any idea that they might come in handy in the near future.

At Hammersmith nick I was told to empty my pockets, which I did, handing over about £100 in cash and my seaman's book. I was given a perfunctory body search and the comb-case was not discovered. Sitting in the cell I began looking at the lock, one of those old-fashioned ones that had a keyhole on both sides of the door.

I started to experiment with one of my double-enders and before long had the cell door open. I crawled along the passageway and peeping through a glass panel I could see the two coppers that had nicked me chatting to the desk sergeant. They seemed engrossed and so I took the opportunity to slide around the corner and amble as nonchalantly as possible along a corridor leading to the main entrance, nodding to two or three Old Bill on the way. It was pouring rain as I walked down the front steps and I finished up standing on Hammersmith high street without a penny piece in my pocket.

There was a trick with the old phone boxes. The receiver rest was a bar about three or four inches long and by tapping out the number on this bar instead of dialling it, you got connected for free. I had a pal living locally who owed me a favour and I rang him to tell him of my predicament. He came around in short order and picked me up, drove me to King's Cross, gave me thirty quid and I caught the train for Scotland and the ferry at Stranraer. That night I was safely tucked up in bed in Ulster.

My next bit of work was in Lisburn, County Antrim. I spent some time casing Boyle's the Jewellers in Market

Square and thought I could open their safe, a Chubb, as easily as I could open a sardine can. My pal Derrick Simmons and I decided to give it a go on the Saturday night. As things worked out we couldn't get in the safe, given its position in the shop and the shop's town centre location, but we captured a fair haul from the display cabinets: rings, watches, chains, gold pen and pencil sets and a few gold lighters. All in all, a total of £4,600.

I went back to London to sell the haul and also because I was keen to try to recover my seaman's book, as the ability to travel anywhere in the world could prove invaluable in my new line of work. An acquaintance called Briggs reckoned he had a crooked Old Bill at Battersea nick and for £800 the man would snaffle it back for me from Hammersmith. I gave Briggs the money and told him to tell the cozzer he could keep the other £100 as well if he could get his hands on it.

The following day I went around to Briggs's house to pick up the book but he'd done the dirty on me. He lived in a cul-de-sac and I drove down and parked. After knocking a few times, I gave up and went back to the car. As soon as I turned out of the cul-de-sac, it was on me: a police car in front and another behind, blocking me in. Being young and fit I took off running and managed to jump on the running board of a passing truck. I pulled a wad of cash from my pocket and waved it at the driver, telling him to drive on. This must have frightened the life out of him because instead of driving on he slammed on his brakes. I leaped off and dashed through a back alley and down a flight of steps, closely pursued by the flat-foots. During the war most iron railings had been removed from public places to be used as scrap for the war effort, often leaving an inch or two of stump. Rounding a corner in my flight I lost my balance and landed squarely with my right knee on one such stump. The pain was excruciating and I bear the scar to this day. Any thought of further flight could be forgotten.

I was taken back to Hammersmith nick. I had a gold pen-and-pencil set on me and in the car the police found a few items from Boyle's. That gave them grounds to get a warrant to search my parents' house. My mother was wearing a three-stone diamond ring I'd given her and in my father's garage they came across the rest of the haul from Boyle's. I was charged with the burglary and my parents were charged with receiving the stolen jewellery. I was remanded to Brixton and my parents were released on bail.

Whilst on remand I got a visit from the Rubber Heel Squad – the internal investigation coppers, or in other words the police who police the police. They started asking me questions about an inspector whose name was Maslin and worked out of Hammersmith. Obviously I wasn't the only one that Briggs had grassed up. I denied all knowledge of the man and it didn't take them long to realise that they wouldn't get far with me.

I blame myself for standing for Briggs. Only months earlier I had bumped into a young East End hard nut called Ronnie Kray in a snooker hall, the first time I'd ever met him, and he marked my card that Briggs was not to be trusted. 'Be careful of the guy you are with,' he said. 'He's a wrong un.' I should have taken more notice.

Bizarrely enough, I was never charged with the Krantz job or with escaping from Hammersmith. People can't escape from a police station without a major inquiry yet in this case there wasn't one, but I was still facing the charge over Boyle's. My big problem was that my parents had been charged with handling, so really I had little choice but to plead guilty. In any case, besides the swag, they'd found key-cutting equipment which would be enough to get me a sentence. A deal was struck whereby the charges against my parents would be dropped in return for the guilty plea.

On 6 March 1956 I was sentenced to three years' porridge, which I spent in Wandsworth Prison, learning everything I could about locks and safes. As I said I was already fairly proficient with my 'double-enders' and there was another little implement known as the 'loid' that I was familiar with. Nowadays in crime films you often see a burglar opening a lock with a credit card. In my day there were no credit cards and in any case I'm not sure they'd be the right tool for the job: too thick and not flexible enough. No, the ideal material was celluloid such as the stuff used in x-ray negatives. Two strips about an inch wide and eight or nine inches long slid into the jamb of a door above and below the lock and shuffled in a sawing motion would have the likes of a Yale open in seconds. My knowledge of safes was the area of expertise that I most wanted to expand.

I had now made a conscious decision which direction my life was going to take. I got friendly with an old boy who was an ex-locksmith and was doing twenty-one months for making a set of keys for a big robbery at London Zoo. Over the years he'd worked for Ingersoll, Chubb and Banham and knew the locksmith game backwards. I haunted him day and night, seeking more knowledge to go with the limited amount I already had and we became good friends. He always said to me, 'Gordon, learn what you can from me while we're here because when I walk out of those gates I never want to see you again.'

When you first go inside for a stretch you don't know anyone, but if you keep your wits about you, by the time you come out you know everyone of any value. Another great source of knowledge was Jim Lightwood, a vastly experienced safe blower and a dyed-in-the-wool villain. He was released a couple of weeks before me and when I got out we teamed up.

I was released on a Wednesday and on the following Saturday Jim and I blew the safe at a dairy company in Chiswick. The £1,900 we escaped with doesn't sound a lot, cut up between the two of us, but back then it was a significant amount. We became quite regular customers at this dairy company, giving their Wandsworth branch a visit on November 5, which seemed a good night to be making a bit of noise. Although we blew the safe we couldn't get it open. The problem was the detonators I was forced to use. The system is known as the 'bum and strum' and has its limitations. A detonator has to be placed in each of the two locks with two fuses which have to be exactly the same length so that the detonators will go off simultaneously, creating one significant 'BOOM'. On this occasion I was sitting on the top of the safe and heard 'boom-boom' and knew we had a problem. The door was jammed shut and there was nothing we could do about it. Had electric detonators been available, no doubt we'd have secured the prize. Still, not to worry, Christmas was only around the corner and the receipts were sure to be bigger that week. Sure enough, on our return visit we cut the back off their recently replaced safe, a cheap secondhand one, and we were delighted to find there was four grand in it. Happy Christmas!

Walking up to my mother's house, where I was living at the time, it was great to see my old mongrel dog sitting in the window waiting for me. My rural upbringing had meant I'd always had a great fondness for animals and Mum reckoned this one knew I was coming from as far away as Hammersmith Bridge and always took up his position at the window to greet me.

JIM AND I HAD our eyes on a post office in Kent but the night we planned to do the job, Jim cried off. He said he'd had a heavy night the night before and was going to a party that night at the house of Charlie Wilson, a top thief who was a couple of years younger than me and came originally from Battersea, south of the river. I knew about the party because I'd been invited myself but felt there was plenty of time for the post office as well. I decided to go it alone, my first solo venture.

Assembling my equipment – gloves, geli, detonators, wires, battery, jemmy and bolt-croppers – I set off for Kent. Removing two of the four window bars and a pane of glass, I was soon inside and began setting the charge. I touched the wires to the battery and nothing happened. I tried again and nothing. I touched the battery to my tongue and realised it was dead. It was very cramped behind the counter where the safe was and hunting for a power point the only one I could find was only about eight feet from the safe, much too close for comfort and anyway I was always nervous of electricity. Then I remembered that when I was parking the car I'd seen an old mattress dumped next to the dustbins in the back alley. I climbed back out and retrieved it, dragging it to the window. It was a life and death struggle getting it through the window but eventually I made it and stuffed it around the safe to make a buffer. Then I inserted the wires into the plug hole.

A tremendous explosion sent me and the mattress flying to the far end of the counter. I must have been unconscious for a minute or two but when I came to my senses, the safe door was hanging open and I began stuffing cash, postal orders and stamps into my holdall.

I arrived at Charlie Wilson's place in plenty of time for a party he had arranged, nine grand richer, though it did take me three or four days to get over the concussion. Charlie and I, along with Bruce Reynolds and Buster Edwards, would go on to be known as the leading lights of the train robbery and the airport robbery. Charlie was a top man and would remain a lifelong friend.

I first met Buster Edwards purely by chance one Sunday evening when I was at the Palladium to see Sammy Davis Junior. About five minutes into the show there was a bit of a disturbance caused by two couples arriving late. It turned out to be Buster and his wife, June, and two friends. Sammy good-naturedly stopped his act to ask the reason for their late arrival and then said they had missed some good stuff, so he had better start again. Which he did. After the show I got talking to Buster in the bar and this was to be the start of another lifelong friendship. Obviously we didn't introduce ourselves to each other as thieves and robbers – these things only became apparent gradually – but we would soon find plenty of common ground and we were destined to do a lot of work together.

Life was pretty much one long social whirl back then. When I wasn't out stealing anything that wasn't nailed down, I was out wining and dining. I wore hand-made shirts from Frank Foster's in Clifford Street, Italian shoes and suits from Toby Benjamin in Savile Row, and spent my evenings in the pubs and clubs that were booming. The Bagatelle on Cork Street and the Log Cabin were very popular venues. Dining out was pretty much a nightly occurrence and I patronised most of the better restaurants. I was never a big fan of those enormous turn-outs, much preferring a more intimate arrangement. Four or six, maybe eight, people seemed plenty to me, allowing the conversation to flow. Even when it came to drinking, which I did a fair amount of, I preferred a few close pals than those mob gatherings. I drove the latest models of the most prestigious cars and was never short of female company. Unlike a lot of the chaps, one vice I never fell into was gambling. I would risk life and liberty in the quest for readies but backing a horse or playing cards wouldn't enter my head.

Although I frequented pubs and clubs, I didn't do so anywhere near as often as a lot of my friends and colleagues. One of the big disincentives for me was the activity of the Criminal Intelligence Bureau. This was a mob of Old Bill who were tasked with infiltrating pubs and clubs patronised by known criminals and compiling dossiers on them. These dossiers were partly based on fact, such as previous arrests and convictions, and partly on observations made by the CIB They would establish who drank with whom and get to know everybody's line of work.

When a job went off, the investigating officers would go to the CIB and troll though the dossiers looking for likely candidates. If they were reasonably sure a particular person was involved it wouldn't take them long to work out who the probable accomplices were. The game was hard enough without giving the Old Bill that sort of start. By the late fifties I scarcely used the West End at all.

People often find my given occupations – ladies' hairdresser/armed robber – an odd combination. In truth I've never cut a lady's hair in my life but I did have an investment in a salon in Fulham which gave me a visible means of support. These days when people ask what I did for a living I say I was in the removal business, which is about as close to the truth as I'm ever likely to tell.

I was at the salon one afternoon when a Detective Sergeant Taylor put in an appearance, wanting to interview me over the disappearance of the Lord Mayor of London's ceremonial gold chain. Apparently, aside from its intrinsic value, it had great historical importance and a pretty dim view was being taken of its theft by people in high places.

He told me that if it was returned no further questions would be asked but I assured him, quite truthfully, that I had no knowledge whatsoever of the theft. He then said that if it wasn't returned I could consider my being on the streets as borrowed time. Most likely DS Taylor had been running around the manor all day threatening anyone who might know someone who knew someone who might know something about the work. Still, the implication of a possible fit-up did nothing to alleviate my inbuilt paranoia.

The chain was never recovered and weeks later I heard on the grapevine that it was put in the pot and smelted down for scrap, which would have only realised a fraction of its value. Shame really. Had I been involved, which as I say

I wasn't, I may have gone the old ransom-it-back-to-the-insurers route, thereby earning more and the original chain would still be in existence.

SEVERAL OTHER BITS of work followed the post office, sometimes with Jim and sometimes with a few other pals of mine. Then disaster struck. Three of my associates were fitted up. Peter Downs had gelignite planted in a sand bucket outside his apartment, Tommy Clarke had detonators planted behind the bath panelling in his flat and Ray Foster had a torn postal order from the post office robbery planted under the seat of his car, which was amazing since I had done that bit of work on my own and the lads had never been near the postal orders, but the Old Bill had. They were all arrested. When asked if they were still working with 'the big fella' or 'the tall man' – me – they all denied having seen me in an age.

Ray was the only one to get out of the fit-up. The judge allowed the jury to be taken out to inspect his car, which was one of those big, open-topped Ford Zodiacs. It was accepted that anyone could have planted the postal order under the seat and he was acquitted. The other two went to prison.

I spoke to the copper who nicked them at one of their remand appearances and it turned out he was a pal of Maslin, the crooked cozzer from Battersea. He told me I could look on my not being included in the fit-up as payback for keeping my mouth shut with the Rubber Heels over Maslin's skulduggery. Nice to get a bit of appreciation.

The rest of the year I had pretty mixed fortunes. I spent a lot of time sitting on a travelling jewellery wholesaler with Charlie Wilson and Buster Edwards. We decided that the best opportunity to have him was outside a place called the Gem Shop in Tooting, and began making our plans. It was all pretty straightforward. Parking was at a bit of a premium and we'd need two cars. We'd park them up in the early hours, one immediately outside the shop and the other lower down the street. Buster would wait on the corner until he spotted the jeweller and give the nod to Charlie, waiting in the second car. He'd give me, waiting in the first car, a toot and I'd put my indicator on. The jeweller would think what a fortunate chap he was, a parking spot appearing exactly where he wanted to park, and would stop to let me out. As he parked, Charlie, now accompanied by Buster, would draw up alongside, blocking him in, while I pulled up a couple of yards up the street. Charlie and Buster would relieve the jeweller of his suitcase, with me rendering assistance if need be. We'd all pile into the first car leaving the second one where it was, thereby foiling any attempts by the jeweller to give chase should he feel so inclined. Piece of piss.

We knew from our surveillance that the jeweller always arrived between ten and eleven on a Tuesday and one week we were all set to go, with everyone where they were supposed to be.

'Hello Gordon. How's it going?' I looked up to see a bloke we used to refer to as Gentleman Jeeves, a screw from Wandsworth

Bollocks! Nothing for it now but to abort the mission. I passed the time of day with Jeeves, who wasn't a bad chap as it happens, then told him I'd have to be on my way. We'd certainly have to find a new location because even if we left it six months, Jeeves was sure to remember having seen me there and would mark the Old Bill's card. I gave Charlie a toot, he picked up Buster and we went off to dump the cars. That job got left on the back burner and we never did get around to having him.

I had better luck in Chelsea, where Charlie came up with some information about an armoured car. Charlie and I gave it a couple of weeks' obbo and it seemed do-able, so we set about putting a team together. Micky Ball and Roy James would do the driving and myself, Charlie, Buster and a couple of heavies would take care of the three security guards. It all went like clockwork and we escaped with seventy grand.

I missed out on the Westminster Bank job in Clapham. It was a simple jump-up, which can always be a bit hit-and-miss and I didn't really fancy it. In any case I'd made plans to go fishing that day. I'd arranged to rent a boat, as I often did, from Chertsey harbour and was looking forward to it. Charlie and Joey Grey went on the work and got away with nine grand.

Catford dog track was a nice, simple little touch. There was a quite upmarket model of car that had become very popular with people who had a few quid. A bookmaker at Catford dogs was one such person and he'd bought himself one, the Rover 90. There was a quirk with this model whereby the front doors opened left to right and the rear doors opened right to left. I'd invented a sort of clip which, if inserted over the two door handles, made it impossible for the occupants to open the doors. One night a pal and I watched the bookmaker and his clerk throw their money satchel into the boot of the car and get in. We reversed onto their front bumper, jumped out and slipped the clips over the door handles. There's a tool used by panel-beaters known as a slide hammer. The principle is that one end is attached to a dented door panel or wing, a two-foot bar with a T-bar at the end is screwed on and a sliding weight is thrown along the bar, with inertia causing the dented panel to pop back into place. They were also very handy for removing barrels from locks. Once this became known, the buying of a slide-hammer became problematical. However making one yourself was quite simple. After welding a screw to a hexagonal nut, a couple of turns of a spanner had the lock impaled. Then attach the T-bar with its sliding weight, a quick throw of the weight and out pops the barrel of the lock. It was used a lot for stealing cars but it worked equally well on car boots. That's exactly what happened that night and we took £4,000, leaving the bookmaker and his clerk trapped inside their Rover, which now had a flat tyre, making pursuit impractical.

A female Jewish moneylender called Mimi was another who patronised Rover. This time it was even more straightforward since her driver, Cyril, was in on the swindle and provided us with all the information we needed and with a spare boot key. No need for a slide-hammer. This time we left with £6,000, though we did have to give Cyril his corner. These figures, four grand here and six grand there, may seem trivial at today's values but going back to the fifties, when a working man would have been very fortunate to earn anything like £20 a week, they were substantial sums.

3

West End Boys

I FIRST MET Bruce Reynolds when Buster brought him to see me at the Castle pub in Putney. Bruce also brought along his pal Terry Hogan, who knew Charlie Wilson from their days together in Maidstone Prison, where Charlie had done a sentence for possession of stolen property. Terry had grafted with some of the top villains in London, including Jackie Spot and Billy Hill, and would turn out to be as game as anyone I ever worked with. One piece of work he'd been on was the legendary Eastcastle Street Robbery in 1952, when Terry and six others escaped with £270,000 from a Post Office van. It was a colossal amount at the time, worth around £6 million today.

Times were changing and the days of two- and three-man gangs were coming to an end. With advances in security it was often the case that to get a job done people would have to call on other gangs for expertise or manpower. This led to information being exchanged and a sort of co-operative society springing up, with various people and groups inter-mingling. Much of this inter-mingling went on in pubs and clubs. Although we all had a very pleasant evening at that first meet with Bruce and Terry, and seemed to get along very well, nothing concrete was agreed. We parted saying that if something of mutual interest should come along, we'd share intelligence.

Bruce was away doing something when Terry came to me with a suggestion of a likely target at Old Oak sorting office. Apparently a Securicor van delivered around thirty grand wages every week to the pay office and it didn't seem an impossible target. We went for a look.

The only problem I could see was gaining entry with the speed that would be necessary. The door looked pretty formidable but still, if these things were easy everyone would be doing them. We sat on the place for a few days and realised that the office was deserted at weekends and we would have all the time in the world to get in and have a look about. Buster and I went in on the Saturday night without too much difficulty to inspect the door from the inside. The lock had a hasp that instead of going two or three inches into the frame went about a foot into the wall. We removed it and reduced it to a more manageable couple of inches. The hinges looked very substantial too so we removed three of the five screws from each of the four of them. Then, sort of belt and braces if you will, we removed the other two screws and reduced their length by half. A strong gust of wind might well remove the door now instead of the six able-bodied men with a battering ram and half an hour to spare that would have been required previously. It doesn't matter how well reinforced a door is, if the lock and hinges are no good it might as well be made of fog.

This same trick of shortening the hasp was later used in the film *The Great Bookie Robbery*.

Bright and early on the Tuesday morning, Buster, Charlie, Terry and myself were all in position. We watched the Securicor van deliver the sacks of money and one of the clerks securely – ha! – lock the door behind himself. Giving the van a minute or two to clear the scene, we bailed out of the car. Terry took a run at the door and put his shoulder, with his sixteen stone of muscle behind it, to the door and off it flew. The half dozen clerks, who had assumed they were as safe as the Rock of Gibraltar, stood in shocked silence. Myself, Charlie and Buster grabbed the money bags and dashed back to the car where Terry was now ensconced waiting to drive us off. If I was to say the whole thing took two minutes I'd be exaggerating and a very simple thirty grand was in the hod.

It wasn't long before Bruce Reynolds did come up with something of mutual interest. He got some information about an armoured car guard who was interested in getting involved in a bit of mischief. Having someone on the inside is both good and bad. On the good side you can be pretty sure his information will be accurate as regards times, dates and amounts of money. On the bad side you have to remember that you are dealing with, at least ostensibly, a straight person. When a robbery goes off, any robbery, the very first people to come under suspicion are the people handling the money. This guard would have absolutely no experience of dealing with a hostile police interview and, should he break down under interrogation or fall for one of the myriad ruses used by experienced police interviewers, we could all be in the shit. For this reason I was reluctant to meet him, initially anyway, and left Bruce to make the opening overtures.

Bruce is a fairly astute judge of character and when he came back after the first meeting with the guard he was very enthusiastic, having explained the pitfalls of the likely interrogations and thinking the guard seemed staunch enough. Company policy was for the driver and a guard to sit up front with a second guard remaining in the rear with the money, he being the only one who could open the rear doors. However, a bit of cost-cutting had gone on and at that time there was only the driver up front and one guard, who was supposed to remain in the rear but as soon as the van left the depot would join his pal up front. The driver wanted no part in the villainy but wasn't the type of person to risk life and limb defending the company money, so opposition seemed pretty minimal.

We spent a couple of days watching the van leave the depot and following it along its route, looking for a suitable spot to relieve it of its cargo. We found the ideal spot at a quiet crossroads and the work was planned for the following Tuesday, barely a week after the job had been first mooted.

Charlie and I stole some diversion signs from a roadworks and stored them in a van we had parked up near the cross-roads. Bruce tailed the van from the depot and then got his foot down to arrive at the spot a few minutes in front of the van where Charlie, Terry and I were waiting. As the security van reached the crossroads, slowing for the diversion signs, Bruce, contrary to the plan of giving it a glancing blow, rammed it head-on, bringing it to a halt. Rather him than me. Terry and I ripped the doors open and gave the driver and the guard a clump, more for effect than to inflict any injury, while Charlie climbed through to the rear and opened the doors. Forming a human chain, we bundled the cash boxes into the waiting getaway car, leaving the driver and guard dazed but pretty much intact. A couple of miles from the scene we swapped over to a new car, transferred the money and headed into town for a count up. Sixty-eight grand and jolly nice too.

The driver and guard got every bit as much of a grilling as the guard had been led to expect. The police were convinced they were involved and held onto them both for several days but they managed to hold out and were eventually released. A few weeks later Bruce went around and gave the guard his corner.

ONE OF MY great passions was playing snooker and, although I wasn't brilliant and certainly didn't consider myself a gambler, I was prepared to play for a few quid. I used a snooker hall in Putney and got into a routine of playing a bloke two or three times a week for £1 a frame. We'd normally finish up a couple of quid one way or the other, with me winning more often than not. The thing that puzzled me was that he always paid me in old one-pound notes which at the time were in the process of being taken out of circulation. One day I asked him how he came by them, joking that he must have a stash somewhere. He said no, the only place he got them was in his pay packet, which aroused my curiosity. By coincidence I banked at the same branch as this bloke's boss and I knew that when receiving deposits of money the teller always separated the old notes from the new ones and never issued old ones when I made a withdrawal. If this bloke's wages were being paid in old notes they weren't coming from the bank, which meant the boss had a stash of them somewhere. I made it my business to find out where.

All this was happening very much on my own doorstep and if I was seen loitering about near the man's house I'd be the first one turned over in the event of a burglary. It wasn't the sort of job that would need a cast of thousands so I decided to put Bruce and Terry onto it. They put in a bit of time watching the house and working out the boss's routine before making a move one Saturday night. A set of double-enders allowed them access through the front door and they began their rummage in the cellar. In no time they discovered the safe, which they manhandled up to the ground floor and clumped into the boot of a Jag.

Then the phone rang. Peering out through the front room window, Bruce spotted some activity in a downstairs window across the street. Thinking the neighbour had possibly noticed occupants in what should have been a deserted house, any thoughts of a rummage upstairs were forestalled. In any case, thinking they had secured the prize, they decided it was time to make good their escape, so off they went. When we got the safe open we were all highly delighted to find £39,000 inside. A couple of days later my playing partner showed up at the snooker hall and began to tell me a story about how his boss had been burgled over the weekend. He went on to say how fortunate the boss had been because the burglars missed the bulk of the money which was in an upstairs wardrobe. If losing thirty-nine grand can be looked on as a winning turn God alone knows how much was missed in the upstairs bedroom.

I HAD A Spanish pal, Pepe, who had got his girlfriend into trouble and was desperately seeking some assistance. I knew a doctor who, for a small consideration, would perform an abortion. A lot of people did know such a doctor in those days. In return the friend gave me some very useful information about an Italian restaurateur who kept large sums of money in his house. He couldn't tell me exactly whereabouts in the house but assured me that it was there. I sat on the man for a few days and got to know his routine, which was to arrive home around seven in the evening. The problem was how to get his wife out of the house for an hour or so to give us a chance to ransack the place. She never seemed to leave.

I recruited a pal. We dressed him up in chauffeur's uniform and acquired a limo for him. He then went around to the house saying he was from the hospital, the husband had been involved in a minor accident, would be kept in overnight and would his wife be good enough to prepare a toilet bag and some pyjamas and accompany the chauffeur to the hospital. We chose a hospital some distance away and by the time she had made all her fruitless enquires there was no way she'd be back inside an hour and a half. Bruce and I gained access to the house and began our search. After about forty-five minutes we struck gold, finding two biscuit tins in a cupboard under the stairs containing three grand.

Another nice bit of work was a greengrocer on the Upper Richmond Road who also kept a fair stash of readies. This time I knew exactly where to find his stash and decided to go in during the night. He lived in a first floor flat over a parade of shops on a busy road so it wasn't going to be easy. I managed to get a ladder up to a window at the side and, it being summer, found the window partly ajar. Crawling into the bedroom, I slid under his bed and found the money, coincidentally in biscuit tins. I made my getaway with eleven grand.

It may seem implausible that I was fortunate enough to find so much cash just lying about but you have to remember the climate of the time. During the war and throughout the post-war years, rationing had been in force and the black market was thriving. Butchers, bakers, greengrocers, publicans and restaurant owners couldn't survive without dealing with the local spivs, one of whom could be found in most local pubs. All these transactions were based on cash. Having bought your stock through the back door, it was impossible to declare the income from it so it couldn't be banked. The only place to keep it was under the mattress, but people talk. Staff, customers, disgruntled ex-lovers, estranged wives were all in a position to do a bit of gossiping and often did. These were the kind of sources from which a lot of my information came. To a certain extent it still goes on today. Independent businessmen, the likes of market traders, who work cash to stock and stock to cash, make every effort to avoid the scrutiny of the tax man and the dreaded VAT man. Bookmakers are another prime example. It's perfectly routine procedure for a bookmaker's clerk to register a £1,000 bet as a tenner with a couple of dots after it, thereby accruing a 50p tax liability instead of a £50 one. Do this a couple of times a day and you could be nicking a monkey a week, or £25,000 a year, off the tax-man. This money can't be banked but rather has to be stuffed under the mattress and reserved for life's little luxuries like Caribbean cruises and the odd jaunt down to the local brothel.

Don't get me wrong, it wasn't a licence to print it. Although I had a fairly lucrative time, for every good tip I got there could be half a dozen fruitless ventures on which I would waste days or even weeks.

For example, I had a lady friend – I had several at a time in those days – who worked as a secretary for a wholesale jeweller on Park Lane. One night, working late and probably to impress her – she wasn't a bad sort – he opened the safe and showed her a sample case containing what she described as a huge amount of unset gemstones. Shortly afterwards she came and told me that he was relocating to his estate in Bognor and had had the safe moved there, presumably with the stones inside. Bruce went on a scouting mission to Bognor library to check the electoral roll, finding his address and the fact that the only residents were the jeweller and his wife. Bruce, Buster and myself went down to look the house over, taking Roy James with us as the driver.

We had the use of a caravan and spent a few nights giving the house our usual professional scrutiny but the residents seemed to do little socialising and the place never appeared deserted. Since there were only the two of them and given its secluded location, we decided on a night-time entry and a tie-up. One early morning we were about to make our entry via a downstairs window when Roy gave us a whistle that something was afoot. It turned out to be the local plod cycling down the lane. He dismounted next to our stolen Jag and started giving it the once-over. He opened the door and spotted the keys in the ignition and removed them, no doubt thinking he was doing a careless local resident a favour. Being the conscientious chap he obviously was, there was sure to be some mention made in his log so we'd have to postpone. We set off back to London but four men driving through West Sussex in a Jag at three in the morning is a bit conspicuous and at a crossroads a police patrol car pulled out behind us and turned on his blue lights. An Old Bill driving a Rover versus Roy James driving a Jag was no contest and although they gave it their best shot, chasing us halfway home, we managed to evade them and abandoned the car in the London suburbs.

A few weeks later we were back and on this occasion we did gain entry, only to be confronted by the harridan that was the jeweller's wife who gave us a venomous volley of abuse, finishing up by saying in any case we were wasting our time, the gear was no longer in the house. Nonetheless we tied the pair up and set about opening the safe, only to find she was telling the truth and the cupboard was bare. I'm not a vicious person by nature but I could have cheerfully strangled the old bitch. By now I was like a dog with a bone and after further enquiries I discovered that they owned another home at Cap Ferrat on the Riviera. I was determined to pay that place a visit but by now there was a distinct lack of enthusiasm amongst the troops and eventually that bit of work died a death.

ONE JOB THAT got away will haunt me for the rest of my life – it could have been a massive touch. We'd had a tip that the Bank of Ireland in Cork City looked very vulnerable and had nothing in the way of overnight security personnel. Buster, Gus Brown and myself went over to have a look and it did look to be for the taking. We spent a few nights observing it and on one of the nights, sitting in a café across the street, I saw a man exit the bank and pause to light a cigarette. When he walked on, I slipped out and started to tail him. He went into a pub and ordered a pint and a sandwich. I waited an hour or so until he was ready to leave, then followed him as he went back to the bank and let himself in. So much for no night security. We kept our eyes on him the next night and the next and the next and it was the same procedure each night.

By the fourth night I'd decided it was time I had a look inside the place and I now knew I had an hour in which to do so. I broke into an adjacent solicitor's office and made my way to the roof and from there to the roof of the bank. I prised open a skylight and lowered myself about twenty feet to the bank floor by means of a rope and wandered down to the vaults to have a look at the safe. It was a Hobbs and safes don't come much easier to open than a Hobbs. There was also a Chubb night safe which it would be a shame to leave untouched. Given its position, opening it with the oxy-arc was not on but there are other ways of opening a safe. I was delighted. Getting down the rope had been difficult enough but trying to get back up it was out of the question, so I left by the main door leaving Buster and Gus to haul up the rope and meet me back at the pub.

We were going to need some materials, not least of all gelignite and detonators, but I had a good idea where I could get them from. We had three hideouts, or stows as we used to call them: one in Waterford, one halfway between Waterford and Cork at Youghal and one in Donegal in the north-west, just in case of emergencies. Not far from Youghal was a quarry where I was sure we could get the explosives, so we went off to burgle it. We got the geli handy enough, stored in a steel cabinet, but the detonators were more troublesome. They were in a Chubb safe and I didn't have the means to open it. There was nothing for it but to go back to England and get the detonators in London.

I bought a racing bike and inserted five detonators inside the frame. Dressing myself up in peaked cap, sports shirt and those things like plus-fours that bikers wear, I booked on a flight from Heathrow to Cork. Buster pissed himself when he saw me coming through arrivals dressed like that and carrying my bike. I'd also organised the transportation of an oxy-arc burner in case we had to cut the safe open.

The plan was for the three of us to go in on the Saturday night by means of the skylight while the night man was on his break. When he returned we'd tie him up and then have the rest of the night to take care of business.

Things began to go wrong a few days before the planned robbery. Buster drove me into Cork from the stow at Youghal because I wanted to leave a suit at the cleaners. He dropped me outside the cleaners and for some reason I turned back in the doorway to say something to him and saw a bloke leaning in the car window talking to him. Next thing he got in the car with Buster. I shouted over to ask if he was alright. He said he was. It turned out the bloke was from the car hire company and either the rental or the insurance had expired and he wanted Buster to come with him to the office and bring things up to date. As luck would have it the rental office was next door to the police station and as Buster was leaving he was arrested by two detectives.

We had a prearranged spot to meet if anything untoward happened but Buster never showed up. Mid-afternoon we were hanging about around the courthouse when Buster walked down the steps. He tipped us the wink not to speak to him and so we followed him at a distance. Eventually we reassembled in a pub and Buster brought us up to date on developments. With all the delays we'd evidently become conspicuous and the Old Bill had got suspicious. They told Buster they knew exactly what he was up to, which I'm sure was untrue but they knew it was something. They also said they knew who he was, which was probably also untrue since he had false ID in the name of North. They also told him they knew where he was living, which they may well have done because we'd been obliged to park the hire car in the lane outside the cottage. Buster hadn't been charged with anything but they gave him twenty-four hours to get out of the country.

We had no choice but to abort another mission, and set off back to Youghal to do a spot of tidying up. The oxy-arc would have to go. Halfway through the clear-up, two police motorbikes drove up the driveway and we lay on the floor behind the furniture. One copper dismounted and came and banged on the door a few times and had a bit of a peep through the window, but seeing no movement and getting no reply he remounted and the pair rode off. We dismantled the oxy-arc, which is an enormous piece of equipment, the most valuable and difficult part to acquire being the gun. This I carefully wrapped in oilskin and buried in the garden. The carcass of the machine we manhandled down to a swamp at the end of the garden and watched it disappear into the mire.

BACK IN LONDON it was fairly common knowledge that vast amounts of money travelled all over the country on trains. I had a pal, Tommy O'Malley, who'd been quietly getting a good living grafting, mainly at Euston Station. He had a suitcase with a false bottom which he would slide over an unattended suitcase, picking it up and making his escape. It was a bit hit-and-miss but he had several decent touches and was the first person to mention the Irish mail train that left Paddington every week. He convinced me that it carried a lot of mail posted by Irish construction workers sending money home to their families. The secret of success was information. Getting your hands on the money required finding out where it was leaving from and where it was going to, and we did get hold of some good info. There was a train that left from Paddington carrying the payroll for rail workers in Swindon which sounded like something worth taking a look at. Buster and I went to Paddington several times and eventually spotted seven steel boxes being loaded into the guard's van. We boarded the train for a recce of a suitable spot to stop it and remove the boxes – security was too tight at Paddington and Swindon – and found what we needed. It was an abandoned factory near West Drayton, quite near the rail line and with plenty of room to park up a couple of cars. We thought we'd have a dummy run at stopping the train at the right spot. Stopping trains at right spots was a problem that would come back to haunt me.

The only system we knew of was pulling the communication cord so we thought we'd give it a try. Buster and Bill Jennings boarded the train whilst I drove out to West Drayton and the factory to wait and pick them up. Bill locked himself in the toilet with Buster waiting outside. Two hundred yards from the factory, Bill pulled the cord and lo and behold the train screamed to a halt virtually right outside the doors of the factory. They disembarked, ran to the waiting car and off we drove. This bit of work certainly looked do-able.

On the day of the robbery, Bruce, Bill, Buster, Charlie and myself boarded. I was carrying a jemmy to gain access to the guard's van and as soon as the train left Paddington we'd break in and tie him up. At the appointed spot Bill would pull the cord and then come and help us manhandle the seven or eight boxes to the waiting van, which was driven by Dennis Marlowe and would be waiting at the factory. All went well, the guard was tied up, I forced the sliding van doors ready to unload the boxes and the cord was pulled at the exact spot as before.

However, this time nothing happened. The train hurtled on. Buster, now in the guard's van with us, spotted a big wheel which he guessed was a brake and began spinning it but the train rattled on another four or five hundred yards past the factory before coming to a halt. Lugging these boxes twenty yards was one thing but trying to hump them four or five hundred yards was another thing altogether. To make matters worse, a gang of navvies working on the line saw what was happening and began throwing rocks at us. First one box was discarded, then another. Dennis, thinking the job had gone boss-eyed, began to drive away, fortunately in the same direction we were running. He stopped to pick us up and by that time the only person left with a box was me. One box.

When we got home and forced it open, it contained the princely sum of £700.

ONE DAY, CHARLIE Wilson came to see me.

'You interested in a bit of work?' he asked.

'Yeah, sure. Where and when?' I replied

'Shepherd's Bush. Half four this afternoon. About an hour's time.'

'Nothing like a bit of notice, is there.'

The job was at the television studios on Scrubs Lane where the payroll was about to be delivered. Me, Charlie and a couple of pals of his set off, pausing only to collect my stocking mask, knitted cap and weapon of choice, a Spanish Guardia Civil truncheon, a flexible thing made of leather and rubber. I carried this partly because it had been a sort of lucky mascot on previous occasions and partly for humanitarian reasons: it was more of a frightener than a deadly weapon. It would certainly sting a bit if you got a clump from the leather-coated baton but it would be much less damaging than from a metal bar.

We entered the building, me wearing the cap with the stocking rolled up underneath. Charlie had obtained the password for the payroll office and we headed straight there. On the way we passed a security guard, who gave us a bit of a looking at but said nothing. Giving the password, we were admitted to the office and ordered the clerks to the floor. We began stuffing trays of pay packets into a couple of holdalls but I noticed a pair of hands clinging to the wooden partition and next minute the head of the security guard at the glass window above. He'd smelt a rat and was peeping through to see what was going on. There was nothing for it but to take what we had, make our excuses and leave. There were still stacks of money in a corner that hadn't yet been put in pay packets and we probably left more behind than we stole but that's life. We still managed to escape with about forty grand, which is a healthy enough figure for a spur-of-the-moment job.

The pantomime at West Drayton hadn't put us off the idea of trains. On the contrary, we all agreed how unfortunate we'd been on that turn-out. Had the train stopped where it had stopped on the dummy run, we'd have all been several thousand quid richer. Perhaps the answer was stealing the money while it was being loaded or unloaded, or immediately before or after.

Buster got a tip about a payroll that arrived for the staff at Brixton station and we went to have a look at the procedure. We spent a couple of week on observation, checking out their schedule. Leaving the bank, the couriers had to pass through an underpass and that was the spot we thought best to have them. Buster entered the underpass from one end and Harry from the other whilst I waited in the getaway car. Midway through the underpass, one of the couriers was given a clump and the other threw himself to the floor. Grabbing the bag, the lads joined me in the car and we departed with four grand. I dropped them at a second car and then wandered off to hail a cab. I told the cabbie to take me to Brixton town hall but unfortunately he took the same route I had taken from the station. I found myself in a traffic jam caused by an ambulance picking up the injured courier. Through the open cab window I heard one courier asking the other if the robbers had got the money. It took me all my powers of self-control not to shout, 'Yes, thank you.'

Another little touch was a Turkish cigarette warehouse in Parsons Green. It was a massive struggle selling the smokes, a brand called Tafani that no-one had heard of. We did eventually get out of them and made a few grand.

A car dealer I knew in West London had been involved in a hire purchase scam with his ex-partner. At the time there were very stringent HP restrictions and by law a buyer was obliged to pay a one-third deposit. However a little bit of creativity with the figures could reduce or eliminate the tiresome deposit. It was totally illegal of course but you could sell a lot more cars than your rival around the corner who followed the rules.

For this reason the ex-partner kept fairly substantial amounts of money at his home in Ascot. Buster and I decided to relieve him of some. After a few days' surveillance we gained entry one evening and found a small safe rag-bolted to the floor. Blowing it open, we discovered £6,500 and the key to a second safe, which we found in the bedroom. This safe only contained some cheap jewellery but all in all it was a very pleasant evening's work.

Charlie put up a bit of work at the butchery business he worked for on Northcott Road. It seemed quite good because we could be absolutely sure of how much would be there and where the safe would be. The noise of blowing it would have been a problem, so we thought we'd take it away and open it at our leisure. We managed to bundle it out as far as the van but struggled to lift it high enough to get it inside. You generally only get one go at these things and if you don't get it right first time you'll never get it in. We gave up at the third attempt and left the safe sitting on the pavement. We were doubly frustrated because we knew there was £4,000 in it. I walked back past the place half an hour later and watched glumly as a crane lifted it onto a lorry. Can't get them all right.

4

The London Airport Robbery

CHARLIE WILSON WAS the one who came up with the information on the Heathrow airport job and it was more than slightly interesting. BOAC, which later amalgamated with BEA to become British Airways, had their head-office at Comet House on the far side of the runways from the passenger terminals at Heathrow, or London Airport as it was then. Behind the building there was a chain-link fence with a chained and padlocked gate that gave access to a road leading to the M4 motorway. Some two hundred yards away was a branch of Barclays Bank from which the payroll for the BOAC staff was collected every Tuesday morning. The information, which came from an employee of BOAC, was that we could be talking of something in the neighbourhood of four hundred grand. It certainly wanted looking at. Buster and myself went to do just that.

Security at Comet House was non-existent – not a commissionaire or even a receptionist. Dressed in business suits we wandered around the building with no-one giving us a second glance. Buster took the lift up to the top floor, the sixth, and went into the gents. From the toilet window he had a clear view across the car-park to the bank and stood and watched the whole operation. The payroll, in a strongbox, was loaded into a van and, accompanied by two security guards, was driven from the bank to Comet House. The van was followed by three tellers in a car and occasionally, even though it was only a couple of hundred yard trip, a police escort. No sign of the Old Bill that day. I hung about in the foyer reading a newspaper and watched the strongbox loaded on a trolley and wheeled to the lift. The lift stopped on the first floor, where the wages office was, as the informant had told Charlie.

It looked straightforward enough, the only fly in the ointment being the possibility of the police escort which was something we'd have to look into. We called a meeting to report our findings and select a team. Bruce, Charlie, Buster and myself were already in. We had access to the best two getaway drivers in London in Roy James and Micky Ball. Bill Jennings and Bruce's pal Terry completed the team of eight.

We acquired a couple of Jags and Bill and I went to buy a pair of bolt-croppers for the chain on the gate to the perimeter road which would be our escape route. For some reason the ironmonger didn't fancy Bill, although he was dressed in overalls and looked like the sort of chap who might have the need for such an item. Anyway, he followed Bill out of the shop and jotted down my car registration number. The weekend before the robbery I went and cut the chain on the gate.

The job was planned for November 20 and everyone was on parade for 9am. Micky and Roy, dressed as chauffeurs, were parked up in the two Jags and the rest of us were dressed as city gents. We were all wearing various types of headgear to cover our stocking masks that would be pulled down at the appropriate moment. I'd dyed my hair black, had affixed a false moustache, was carrying my trusty Guardia Civil truncheon and was wearing a tweed hat. Dennis and Bruce were carrying rolled-up umbrellas from which the shafts had been removed and replaced by steel bars.

Charlie, Terry and I took the lift up to the top floor where we were joined by Buster and Bill. Looking out of the toilet window Buster saw the van pull up outside the bank and was about to give Bill the signal to summon the lift when he saw a police car pull up next to the van. All a bit of an anticlimax and we'd have to abort, but not to worry there'd be another Tuesday along in seven days.

The following weekend I drove out to the airport only to find that the chain I'd cut had been replaced. If I cut it again and it was spotted by security they were sure to realise somebody was up to a bit of skulduggery. I took the chain away to the metalworker who had installed the steel bars in the umbrellas and got him to fit a very well-concealed false link. Now it was just a matter of unhitching the chain and we'd be on our way. I went and replaced the chain.

The following week, November 27, was pretty much the mixture as before. Charlie, Terry and myself followed Buster up to the toilet but unlike all the previous visits there was a toilet attendant. We spent what seemed a lifetime washing hands and straightening ties while Buster stood at the urinal trying to make pissing noises. Finally Buster saw the van leaving the bank and this week without the Old Bill escort. We were on. Buster gave the nod to Terry to summon the lift and he held the door open to retain it until it was summoned from the ground floor.

Once inside the lift we pulled our stocking masks down from their concealment under our assorted headgear. This proved a bit embarrassing when the lift stopped at the second floor and we had to rapidly re-conceal them. Fortunately whoever had summoned the lift had given up waiting and had taken the stairs. Once we were moving' the masks were pulled down again only for the lift to stop again at the first floor. This was getting quite disconcerting but once again the lift-summoner had taken the stairs.

Downstairs Bruce and Dennis, in their city gents outfits, had waited in the parked Jags. They'd watched the strongbox unloaded onto the trolley and wheeled into the foyer and followed inside. We eventually descended in the lift and when the doors opened, the guards and tellers were confronted by us in the lift and Bruce and Dennis from behind.

'On the floor and keep your fucking mouths shut,' shouted one of the chaps. If excessive violence is to be avoided it's imperative to seize the initiative from the first seconds. Once security people are convinced that resistance is futile, self-preservation kicks in and the objective is achieved.

It was all over in seconds. The guards were overpowered and two of the tellers dived to the floor whilst the third took a little persuasion. Terry and Bill grabbed the box and ran out to the cars which were now reversing to meet them, slung the box into the boot of Micky's car and dived into the back seat. We all baled into Roy's car and we screeched of towards the chained gate. Charlie and Buster jumped out to remove the false link but it was so well disguised Buster couldn't find it and Charlie ended up having to use the bolt-croppers.

As we were turning out of the gate some busybody spotted something afoot and reversed his Austin A40 to block the gateway. Micky stopped a few yards ahead and Roy swerved around the busybody's banger, brushing it out of the way and shooting past Micky. The traffic lights were just turning red and Roy realised that Micky could well get entangled in the cross traffic. Driving on pure instinct he pulled across the westbound lane, blocking the traffic and allowing Micky to shoot past on his nearside. A truly fantastic piece of driving.

We abandoned the Jags at the lock-up where we were doing the changeover and put the strongbox in a van to be transported to Jimmy White's flat where we were doing the carve-up. The bolt-croppers were left on the seat of the Jag.

Me and Roy had intended to leave by motorbike but we couldn't get it started so I took the Tube home and changed out of my disguise. I was the last to arrive at Jimmy's just as the first news bulletins about the robbery were coming out. By tradition the box had been left unopened until everyone was present. We were due a bit of a disappointment. We'd anticipated around forty grand a man but when we got the box open we were greeted by a total of sixty-two grand. With a share for the bloke who gave the information and a drink to Jimmy for the use of his flat we were left with six grand apiece. Terry was so disappointed that he vowed to give up the game but we all thought he'd get over it when the next bit of work came up.

The problem with working with the two best wheel-men in London was that the police knew exactly who they were as well. Obviously the police were as impressed by Micky and Roy's driving as we had been and they gave them a tug. Also, the list of people that may have been working with them was fairly limited so it was a case of round up the usual suspects. The day after the job they arrested Roy, Micky, Charlie and myself and put us on an identity parade at Cannon Row nick. We were obliged to don bowler hats and affix false moustaches and we looked like two pairs of Laurel and Hardy. No wonder nobody picked us out. The only evidence they found at my place was some theatrical make-up which was nothing like enough to charge me and we were all released.

I followed my usual routine when the heat was on of making myself scarce. I flew to Tangier where I was joined a few days later by Bruce and we enjoyed a couple of weeks in the sun. I decided to take the ferry over to Gibraltar where I was thinking of investing my windfall in a watch smuggling operation that I'd been told about. At the time the Victory brothers were running most of the skulduggery going on in Gibraltar – by and large smuggling of one description or another. During a conversation with one of them in a bar the subject of the airport robbery came up and he said, 'Did you hear how those cheeky bastards flew the proceeds out of Britain on a BOAC flight?' Just shows you how these myths can take hold.

Nothing came of the watch smuggling project and after a week I returned to London, hoping that the heat had died down.

It hadn't. No sooner back in the country than another series of identity parades was ordered, this time at Twickenham. Again the run-around with the hats and 'taches. Then we were told to change into boiler suits and the ironmonger from whom Bill Jennings bought the bolt-croppers was brought in. He wrongly identified Micky, who did look a lot like Bill, as the man who bought them. Micky took this badly. He knew if he was convicted of the violence in the foyer he was facing big bird and he agreed to plead guilty to being the driver. He would later be sentenced to five years. Two people identified Charlie and me and we were charged.

I had a good brief, Brian Field, who Buster and I had used on several other occasions. He was the managing clerk at Wheater & Co. I got hold of him and he succeeded in getting me bail. My first priority was to establish a watertight alibi. If I could prove I was in, say, Soho, at 9.30 on the morning of November 27 then obviously I couldn't have been robbing a security van at Heathrow airport, now could I?

There was a shirtmakers, Frank Fosters, on Clifford Street that I used regularly and he was prepared to say that at precisely that time on that day I was having a fitting at his place of business. When I left the shirtmakers I went to a café bar, the Kardoma, where I accidentally bumped into another customer, spilling coffee on his trousers. It turned out this customer was a retired colonial policeman, so who better for an impartial witness. At the time I owned a ladies' hairdressers and I gave this man my card telling him to have the trousers cleaned and send me the bill. I remembered the specific day because the man had been reading the *Daily Telegraph* newspaper with a front page picture of Khrushchev hugging Fidel Castro. Brian Field placed an advert in the *Telegraph* asking the man to come forward and help prevent an innocent person be wrongly convicted. He was good enough to do so.

The second prosecution witness claimed he had seen me from the upstairs of a bus as I was getting out of one of the Jags at the airport. I got Brian to hire a bus and take a photographer along the route. I had a good pal, Terry

Fincher, who won Press Photographer of the Year four times and who would have been perfect for the job but due to contractual commitments he was unable to take on the work. He did recommend a colleague and the resulting photographs proved the man couldn't have seen what he claimed to have seen.

Charlie's trial only lasted till the end of the prosecution case. Two witnesses had identified him but at different places at the same time. One or both of them had to be mistaken and the judge directed the jury to find him not guilty. My own trial wasn't going so well despite the alibi, which the police were challenging, and anyway several witnesses insisted they could identify me as having been at the airport. There was nothing for it but to try and bend one of the jurors and I began to cast my eye over them trying to spot one that might be responsive to threats or bribes.

Back in the good old days when verdicts had to be unanimous jury nobbling was quite a little cottage industry and there were teams that specialised in assisting defendants to get a member of the jury to co-operate. Threats, bribes or a combination of the two were the order of the day. The rule was you could have a trial and two retrials, after which the judge would tell the prosecution that they were pissing against the wind. So, if you could corrupt one juror in three trials you were sure to walk. Leaving aside the expense, it makes you wonder how anyone ever got convicted.

I had one pal who was up at The Bailey and things weren't going too well but some friends got busy and eventually a susceptible juror was selected. They followed him from court and his first port of call was a betting shop where one of the pals got talking to him.

'Here, aren't you on that jury at The Bailey?' he asked.

'Yes, but I'm not allowed to talk about it,' said the juror.

'No, no. Course not. Just wondering how you thought it was going, what with a pal of mine being on trial and all that.'

There was no reply as the juror continued perusing the card for the next race.

'Fancy anything,' asked the pal.

'Number three looks to have a chance,' replied the juror.

'There you go mate. Have a few quid on it from me,' he said stuffing five hundred quid in the juror's inside pocket.

The following morning the juror arrived in court wearing a nice new blazer and his shirt still had creases where it had just come out of the box. He squeaked his way over to the jury-box in his new brogues, obviously having treated himself to a bit of new clobber with his little windfall. With all the winks and thumbs ups coming from the juror the defendant was forced to excuse himself from the dock, claiming an upset stomach, before everyone in the court smelt a rat. The verdict was satisfactory.

Of course, try as they might, the jurynobblers couldn't always get to one of the jurors but there was another little ruse known as 'a rick and a mistrial'. Whilst you could have only one trial and two retrials you could have an unlimited number of mistrials. The most common reason for a miss-trial is that something is disclosed to the jury that they shouldn't know about. If a witness, preferably a prosecution witness, can be coerced into accidentally letting something slip it's a massive problem for the judge.

Supposing a witness could be persuaded to say something like 'Yes, well I had my doubts about Mr Smith because of all the other times he's been nicked. Oops, shouldn't have said that, should I?'

No matter how much the judge admonishes the jury to disregard the remark you can't unring the bell. If he allows the case to continue the defendant will have pretty substantial grounds for appeal and there's little option but to order a retrial. This means a new jury and a second bite of the cherry for the jury nobblers.

I see nothing wrong in principle with jury nobbling, preferring to look on it more as levelling the playing field. The whole jury system is weighted very heavily in favour of the prosecution. It's often said that a jury is a group of twelve people too stupid to avoid jury service and these people automatically assume that the police know what they're doing. They believe the accused wouldn't be in the dock if he wasn't guilty and will go on believing it until they hear concrete evidence to the contrary. So, those old maxims like 'innocent till proven guilty' and 'the onus of proof is on the prosecution' are nothing short of utter bollocks.

Of course nowadays with judges being able to accept a ten to two majority verdict the nobblers need three corrupted jurors to be sure of a hung jury. Makes the whole thing that much more impractical. And expensive.

I made my selection and at the end of the day tailed him home to his house in Finchley. Buster and I returned that night but got no answer to our knocking. The next morning I parked up along the street from the man's house and waited for him to leave for court.

Pulling up next to him I said, 'What a small world! Off to court? Hop in, I'll give you a lift. I'm going to The Bailey myself.'

He didn't seem too perturbed by the encounter and we chatted away for a few minutes. Eventually I got to the point.

'How do you see the result going?' I asked him.

He didn't answer for a minute or two, just stared out the window. Then he said something that was enough to make me believe in Santa Claus and the Tooth Fairy.

'I've done a bit of bird myself, you know.'

It couldn't happen today, what with all the jury-vetting and stuff that goes on, but I really couldn't have wished for a better bit of luck.

I slipped him £500 and told him there'd be another good drink if he came back with a not guilty verdict. That was a bit too much to hope for but a hung jury and a retrial would suit me fine.

The judge finished his summing-up and sent the jury out, reminding them of the need for a unanimous verdict. They returned two or three times saying they were deadlocked and in the end the judge dismissed them and ordered a retrial. We lived to fight another day.

THERE WASN'T MUCH chance of getting such a stroke of luck at the second trial, so the answer had to be a bit of jiggery-pokery with the evidence and the witnesses. The landlord of my flat was an actor and he agreed to say that the make-up found in the flat was his. In fact the second trial was delayed a few weeks because the actor was away in Istanbul playing a role in the James Bond film *From Russia with Love*. The evidence of the man on the upstairs of the bus was pretty much compromised by the photographs and I'm inclined to believe the man was making a genuine mistake.

The most damning witnesses were the ironmonger and the man who claimed I was the one who hit him in the melee in the foyer.

The prosecution's forensics expert had made a great song and dance out of how the cut marks on the chain were definitely made by the bolt-croppers found in the abandoned Jag. If Micky Bell bought them and I was with him in my car it was very damaging because Micky had already pleaded guilty to being the driver. As it happens Micky hadn't bought them, Bill Jennings had and he hadn't been charged. On the day the ironmonger gave his evidence he repeated his conviction that it was Micky he had sold the bolt-croppers to. But then it was time for the defence cross-examination. Bill, dressed in the same boiler suit he had worn on the day he bought the bolt-croppers, was sitting in the front row of the court. The ironmonger did a double take when he saw him. He was now no longer sure it was Micky who was the buyer and his evidence was discredited.

The other witness was going to be the hardest nut to crack. Charlie, Buster and myself went to pay him a visit. I couldn't be seen to be tampering with a witness and Charlie was a bit short in the diplomacy department so Buster was elected to go and speak to the man. He went and knocked on the door and the man's wife let him in. Buster's appearance didn't come as a surprise and the man said he was going to phone his brother who would come and speak to Buster. They agreed to meet in a pub around the corner and Buster came back to bring us up to date. It was all a bit nerve-racking. For all we knew the phone call could be a coded message to tell his brother to phone the Old Bill and charges of conspiracy to pervert the course of justice could be flying about any minute. We decided to front it out and Buster went off to the pub to confront the brother.

'Look we don't want any trouble but my brother has already given evidence at the first trial. If he changes it now he could be nicked for perjury.'

'We're not here to cause trouble and we don't want your brother to change his evidence. All we want him to do is add one line to what he's already said, and there'll be a good drink in it for both of you,' Buster told him.

'We don't want your money, we just want this over with. What do you want him to add?' asked the brother.

'We want him to say that if Gordon Goody was the man in the tweed hat, then he was the man who hit him.'

'Nothing more?'

'No, that's it.'

They reached agreement.

Charlie had got hold of a crooked copper who had access to the prosecution exhibits, one of which was a tweed hat that had been worn by one of the robbers and had become dislodged during the melee in the foyer. For the trifling sum of two hundred quid he was prepared to steal the tweed hat and replace it with an identical one, three sizes bigger. The witness gave his evidence exactly as he had at the first trial, adding the rider about the hat. The prosecutor's bum had hardly touched his chair when my QC was on his feet.

'And if Mr Goody wasn't the man wearing the tweed hat?' he asked.

'Then it wasn't him who hit me,' was the reply.

I was asked to try on the hat and it fell down around my ears and eyes. All very reminiscent of the O.J. Simpson trial. If the hat don't fit you must acquit. The jury was back with a not guilty verdict in pretty short order. I was walking on air as I left the court having just cheated my way out of a fifteen-year sentence, and this was the moment I chose to drop the biggest bollock I've ever dropped in my entire criminal career.

The prosecuting counsel, Michael Corkery, who at the time was the number one Crown Prosecutor, walked up to me, shook hands and congratulated me on the verdict, probably taking the view you win some you lose some. He was holding the cigar box with the make-up which he was about to return to me and over his arm he had the chain from the airport gate.

'Your forensic man wasn't that good was he?' I asked, taking the chain from around his neck. 'He never noticed the false link.' I then opened the link and showed him how the chain came apart. I'm ashamed of myself. As if I hadn't put the Old Bill's and the prosecutors' backs up enough with the not guilty, now I was taking the piss. This act of bravado would come back to haunt me in the not too distant future.

In the meantime it was back to work and we were still convinced that the biggest prizes with the least security were the parcels of cash being carried on a regular basis by train. We had some decent touches though not the mega prizes we all dreamed of.

Bruce and Terry had a bit of a tickle up in Birmingham. They got a tip about a small bookmaking chain that took football bets on behalf of William Hill. On a Friday the coupons and the money were sent by train to William Hill's head office in London. They tailed the van from the betting office to Redditch station. Terry boxed the van in while Bruce simply walked up and snatched the mailbag from the seat next to the driver. Leaving the car where it was they sped off in a second car netting themselves three grand in the process. As I say, a nice little tickle but it got us to thinking. If one small chain was sending three grand, how much was arriving from all over the country? Given the logistics, it would all have to be arriving on a Friday since, in those days, all league football matches kicked-off at three o'clock on a Saturday afternoon.

Me and Buster plotted up outside William Hill's head office at the Barbican while Charlie, Bruce and Terry loitered around Euston. We tailed a couple of vehicles fruitlessly but shortly after lunch we spotted an estate car with two blokes in it leaving the company car park. Sure enough, it headed straight for Euston and we watched as thirty mailbags were loaded into the car. I spotted Bruce, Charlie and Terry watching the same operation from the adjacent platform. If there was three grand in one mailbag we could be talking in the region of a hundred grand in thirty of them. Things looked promising.

During the week we travelled several times over the route from Euston to the Barbican seeking out a convenient spot for the mischief. We found what looked to be the ideal place at a road junction. Harry would ram the estate car off the road, me and Charlie would brandish our coshes to discourage intervention from the passengers whilst Bruce and Buster opened the rear door with a slide-hammer and transferred the sacks to a waiting van. We'd all bale into the van and off we'd go. Seemed a piece of cake.

Fortunately, before Friday came around, Bruce was in contact with his man in Birmingham. Apparently, although the Birmingham chain sent cash, most of William Hill's other clients sent cheques. Even if the raid was a success we'd probably only finish up with thirty mailbags full of football coupons and worthless cheques. Another aborted mission but such is the life of an armed robber.

The two essential ingredients for success are good information and reliable associates. On one bit of work at Isleworth me and Buster had neither. We were stuck for a driver and took on someone with a less than proven track record. The information was, once again, mailbags this time coming into Isleworth station in the early morning hours. We snatched seven mailbags and threw them to the bottom of the station steps but when we followed them down there was no sign of the car or driver. Shouting for the driver we heard the car starting up two streets away. Taking a sack each we ran for the car and were lucky to get away without getting nicked. To make matters worse there was nothing of any value in the two bags. Years later Charlie would tell me that the driver finished up being a grass. Sometimes things are just not meant to happen.

BRUCE HAD A pal, Geordie, who worked as a porter at Waterloo Station. He was fond of a gargle and over a few drinks Bruce managed to extract a couple of gems of information. There were two trains that arrived at Waterloo every week known as the Gold Train and the Money Train, both of which were greeted by very heavy police security. The Gold Train carried a ton of gold that arrived at Southampton from South Africa and the security at Southampton was every bit as heavy as it was at Waterloo. From the station it was taken, under escort, to the Bank of England so if it was going to be intercepted it would have to be done en route.

Bruce and his brother-in-law, John Daly, went down to Southampton to watch the *Union Castle* being unloaded of its cargo. A container was hoisted from the hold by crane and deposited on a security coach at the rear of a train. The coach was locked and sealed and a security guard took up position in the second last carriage which meant the gold, to all intents and purposes, was unguarded whilst the train was in motion.

Meanwhile, Charlie, Buster and I were waiting for the train's arrival at Waterloo. The security was as heavy as Geordie had described it with several dozen Old Bill and numerous railway officials. Taking the gold at the station was a non-starter just as much as taking it at the docks was. The prize was too exciting for the job to be dismissed but the physical drawbacks to unloading a ton of gold on some railway embankment were something we'd have to give a bit of thought to.

For the time being we decided to concentrate our efforts on the Money Train. This train left Bournemouth every evening, picking up sacks at stations en route with Tuesdays being the day of the bumper crop. Its last stop before Waterloo was at Weybridge and with the security at Waterloo this would be the best place to have it. Bruce and John went to give the place a look over.

The train was due to arrive at three in the morning and they were there by two, parking their car on the far side of the old Brooklands racetrack and walking across fields to an embankment above the station. They had a clear view of the station and the platforms and Bruce, being Bruce, began to take notes. At about twenty to three a police car pulled into the station, did a circuit of the car park and drove off, returning a couple of minutes later when the two Old Bill got out and began to chat. Five minutes later a second police car arrived and parked on the far side of the platform. Where they were parked their headlights were shining directly at the spot where Bruce and John were ensconced so they were getting a bit concerned that their presence had been detected. Although as yet they'd done nothing wrong, if they got a pull the whole job was in the dustbin, but they had little choice but to lie low and await developments.

At about ten to three a post office lorry pulled into the station and two postal workers got out and started chatting to the Old Bill. This was all very strange. If, as we supposed, the lorry contained sacks full of money why was everyone performing like they were out for a picnic? The mystery was solved when the train arrived. The lorry wasn't delivering money to the train, it was collecting money from the train. And, given the amount of security, quite a lot of it.

We were now going to need a fair sized team and a lot of surveillance but manpower was no problem. By this time there was Bruce, his pal Alfie Thomas, John Daly, Jimmy White, Charlie, Buster and myself with Roy James to do the driving. Terry was still brooding over the disappointment of the airport job and the work since hadn't been spectacular enough to sway him from his decision to turn the game in. He said his heart just wasn't in it any more. Micky Ball was in doing his five but we had more assistance should the need be. We split into teams of two and kept the station under the microscope.

The following week Buster and I tailed the convoy and it finished up at Weybridge main post office. This place had a fair amount of staff and the local Old Bill seemed to pop in and out on a pretty regular basis so, if it was going to be done, the station yard was the place to do it where we knew what we were up against. Jimmy came up with a suggestion that a combination of fuller's earth and compressed air sprayed into the police cars would knock out the crews leaving just the postal workers to contend with.

We'd progressed as far as renting a lock-up, stealing a couple of Jags and acquiring the compressed air cylinders and fuller's earth when the fickle finger of fate intervened. Something very big came up and Weybridge went on the back burner.

5

Something Very Big

ONE OF THE many misconceptions about the Train was that the airport job was done to finance it. Not true. In the first place the airport work went off on the 27 November 1962 and the first whisper of the Train, which came to me, didn't arrive until 6 May 1963. In the second place, the expenses for the train were pretty minimal and we all had plenty of money.

The original information came from my brief, Brian Field. Actually that's not quite correct. Brian wasn't a fully-fledged solicitor, he was managing solicitor's clerk to a fairly incompetent solicitor called John Wheater and as such had a completely free hand in dealing with the clients. He was much more ambitious than Wheater, living in a much nicer house than his boss and driving a much nicer car. Also, for a person who was part of a profession noted for its integrity, he was totally devoid of scruples. As I said earlier, without his help – having the hats swopped and concocting the alibi – I would undoubtedly have been convicted of the airport job so I had no hesitation in listening to whatever information he had come by.

Stealing money is as easy as falling off a log but a robber's success is directly proportional to the accuracy of his information. Before you can steal the money you have to know where it is. The first meeting was at Brian's offices at the Old Bailey and it was very much a bare-bones outline: if I wasn't interested then the less I knew the better for all concerned.

'I've got something you might be interested in,' Brian told me.

'Oh yeah. What's that?' I asked.

'It's a lot of money that has to be taken in transit. It will require quite a large, well-organised gang and I can introduce you to someone that can give you all the information that you need. Are you interested and are you capable?'

'Course I'm interested and you know damn well I'm capable. When can I meet your contact?'

A second meet was arranged at Finsbury Park, to which I brought Buster. Brian brought a man called Mark to whom I took an instant dislike. He was a supercilious prick with one of those affected public school accents and he got my back up from the moment I met him. However this didn't diminish my interest in the project. Brian also brought a well-dressed man in glasses who to this day has only ever been known as 'the Ulsterman'. On the day he was introduced as 'Freddie', which was clearly not his real name. He was apparently a postal worker employed on the Travelling Post Office, a type of mail train where the post was sorted en route. Like myself he had been raised in Northern Ireland, so although he was quite a bit older than me we had an immediate affinity. By the time we met he had risen to the rank of senior postman and had all the information we needed as to the contents of the High Value Package.

A third meet was held at Marble Arch. By now 'Freddie' had accepted that we were serious people, capable of the work, and he was now a lot more forthcoming. The job was a mail train that left Glasgow each week bound for London carrying mailbags full of surplus cash from the Scottish banks. More mailbags were collected en route and on an average there would be sixty to eighty bags by the time the train reached Euston. At holiday times there might be three or four hundred. Security at Glasgow was very tight, as it was at Euston, so the money was going to have to be taken in transit.

I asked the Ulsterman, 'What kind of dough are we talking about?'

He said, 'Well it could be up to five million pounds.'

For that kind of dough I was definitely more than interested.

Yet another meet was held at Green Park in London on a warm summer's afternoon. We just looked like any other small group of mates, sitting on the grass enjoying a bit of sunshine, but our business was deadly serious.

After a while 'Freddie' got up.

'Anyone fancy an ice cream?' he asked.

He wandered off to an ice cream kiosk, leaving his jacket beside us on the grass. In the exposed inside pocket I spotted a spectacle case, so I slipped it out and opened it. I was curious about the guy and it was an opportunity to find out a bit more about him. Inside was an optician's label with an address in Lisburn, Northern Ireland. The prescription was in the name of one Patrick McKenna.

When 'Freddie' returned I pulled him to one side.

'How come you told us your name was Freddie when in fact it's Paddy McKenna?' I asked.

'How the fuck do you know that?' he demanded, looking shocked. 'It was understood that nobody would know my real name.'

He was more than a little taken aback and at that point the whole scheme came close to being aborted.

'All right, all right,' I reassured him. 'Don't worry. We'll just keep it between Buster and me. No-one else will ever know.'

His secret was safe with us and has remained so until this day. But at this late stage I see no harm in naming Paddy McKenna as the so-called Ulsterman. More of this later.

Another little incident happened during this meet that could have brought the project to a screeching halt. At the time Sir Winston Churchill was gravely ill and the general opinion was that he wasn't going to survive. In fact he lived on for another eighteen months but that didn't stop the paparazzi hanging around Downing Street in droves to monitor the comings and goings. Whilst lounging on the grass I heard someone shout my name and looked to see my old pal Terry Fincher strolling over, camera in hand. God knows what Paddy would have thought of our security arrangements had Terry innocently taken a snap of us all together. I jumped up, shook his hand and led him away before he could shoot any compromising smudges.

Paddy had intimate details of timetables and security. The van carrying the money, the High Value Package, was normally the second car from the engine and contained five or six postal workers. The next section of the train was a mobile sorting office with about seventy postal workers sorting the overnight mail. Paddy now reckoned that at holiday periods we could be talking in the region of £6 million. I'll say that again: six million fucking quid. Time to speak to Bruce.

Me and Buster went around to Bruce's flat and we went through the ritual of waiting for the drinks to be poured before beginning the story. Jameson in hand I started to fill Bruce in on the information we had received. I was doing my best not to get carried away and I suppose Bruce was listening with similar feeling. We'd been through these information exchanges numerous times and more often than not they came to nothing. At the end of my monologue I asked Bruce what he thought.

'All sounds fine but how good is the information? Who did it come from?'

'Brian Field,' I told him.

Bruce was impressed. Although he didn't know Brian personally he knew all about the work he'd done for me over the airport job and he knew me and Buster had had dealings with him for years. We all agreed it was certainly worth pursuing and, drinks in hands, we went all over it again a couple of times with Buster throwing in his titbits and all of us asking questions and making suggestions. Eventually we realised we had gone as far as we could go at this stage; there was a great deal of information we still needed and an awful lot of planning was going to be required. I would stay in touch with Paddy McKenna and we'd have another meet in a few days to discuss personnel.

My feelings were that we could probably do the job eight-handed, maybe ten. Me, Buster and Bruce for sure and Charlie would want in. The meet was held in

Buster's flat and Bill Jennings was there when I arrived as were Jimmy White and Alf Thomas. Bruce arrived with Roy James and we got down to business.

The two major areas of discussion were how to stop the train and where to do it. Our only experience of stopping a train was by pulling the communication cord. Mail trains probably didn't have communication cords and even if they did there was no way of getting someone on the train to pull it. No, if we were going to stop it the only way was at a signal but this was something we knew nothing about. Buster came up with a suggestion. He knew a man, Roger Cordrey, who worked with a South London firm that were busy robbing trains. Perhaps they'd tell us how to do it or better still lend us their man.

Buster went to speak to Roger but it was a no-go. They certainly weren't about to mark our card on how they stopped a train and if we wanted access to their man then Roger's whole firm had to be in on the work. We were now beginning to get a bit over-staffed. It wasn't so much the extra number of ways we'd have to cut up the spoils that was the problem – there would be plenty for everyone. It was more the security element that I was worrying about. As things stood we were all people who knew each other, had worked together and trusted each other. Now we were seriously considering bringing in virtual strangers.

On the other hand, we didn't know how to stop a train so if it was going to be stopped we were going to need help from someone. Also, with the thought of seventy postal workers being only a carriage away perhaps a few extra strong-arms wouldn't go amiss. We argued back and forth but finally accepted that we had little choice but to bring the South London people in. Roger arrived at the next meeting at Buster's flat accompanied by Jimmy Hussey, Bob Welch, Tommy Wisbey and Frank Monroe.

We really were going to have to restrict these gatherings to absolutely essential occasions. We were all people that the Old Bill kept a fairly regular eye on and if they spotted such a combination of odd-bedfellows it wouldn't take them long to realise something major was being planned. As far as I could see the reconnaissance work and information gathering were our responsibility and we could compartmentalise it between ourselves. Roger's team had the responsibility of stopping the train and providing any shortfall in muscle. Interminable meets were unnecessary and dangerous.

On the odd occasion when a meeting was unavoidable we found Wimbledon Common was a fairly inconspicuous turnout and we'd meet by the windmill to have a football kick-about. What could be less suspicious than a bunch of twenty and thirty-somethings enjoying a little recreation on a pleasant summer afternoon.

Having decided on the how, the next problem was the where, so Bruce and John Daly were elected to do a spot of reconnoitring. They took the slow train from Euston stopping at every station along the route the mailtrain would be travelling and it was an hour before they began to leave behind the built-up areas and see some open land that could be suitable for their purposes. Bruce wasn't sure exactly what he was looking for but he knew he'd know it when he saw it. He has a sort of instinct for these things. Not far south of Stony Stratford he knew he'd found it. A

B-road, the B488, ran alongside the tracks and, following a bend, disappeared under a bridge beneath the railway. It would take a more leisurely visit by car to be absolutely certain but Bruce was convinced Bridego Bridge was the perfect spot to unload the train.

The nearest spot that Roger could stop the train was at the signals at Sears Crossing a few hundred yards up the track. By uncoupling the engine and High Value Package van and driving it to the bridge we could isolate the rest of the train with its seventy-odd postal workers who would have no reason to realise what was going on. Roy James and Jimmy White went into uncoupling trains practice. They visited Royal Oak sidings at Paddington where they took the opportunity to walk through the deserted HVP carriage and sorting vans to familiarise themselves.

This just left the problem of actually moving the train, which none of us had a clue how to do. What if the driver told us to go fuck ourselves, he wasn't going to move the train? If, no matter what pressure we put on him, he took this stance then the whole job was in the toilet. Roy James, given that he was a mechanic and driver, was convinced that with a little coaching he'd be able to do it but who do you go to for train driving coaching and what possible reason could you give them for wanting to learn?

One night Bruce and I wandered onto a siding at Euston station to see if I could have a go myself. We gained access to a loco and I managed to get the thing started but I realised that even if I managed to get it in motion, when it came to stopping it I would be stumped. We'd already discovered from the fiasco at West Drayton that stopping a train in the right spot was a crucial part of the business.

Then we had a stroke of luck or so it seemed at the time. Maybe, with hindsight, there was nothing lucky about it. Bruce was visiting a pal, Ronnie Biggs, who had been in Borstal and the nick with him. Out of the blue he mentioned a pal of his that he was doing some work for who was a semi-retired train driver who these days only worked in the shunting yards. Bruce asked Ronnie to find out if he could drive an EE Type 3000 locomotive and if he could was he interested in a bit of work for which he would be paid very handsomely. A few days later Biggs met Bruce to tell him the old boy was familiar with the model of train and was keen to be involved. What did they have to do? They? There was no they. All we needed was someone to move the train a short distance for a long drink. And another long drink for Biggsy for the introduction if need be. Biggsy wasn't having it. He could smell money and wanted to be in. So be it, he was in but at least we had a train driver. As normal the decision was arrived at by consensus and without being clever after the event I was one of those opposed as was Roy James and a couple of others. Still, we had no viable option to offer so what could we do?

The next controversy was what to do with the money once we had it. Bruce and I were in favour of a stow, somewhere to hide out for a few days after the job until the heat had died down. I'd rarely worked without one – on the Cork job we had three. Roy James was in favour of ripping the seats out of a few Jags and high-tailing it back to London and home-ground. We had no way of knowing how long we'd have before the balloon went up or how quick the police could set up roadblocks. Hurtling down country back roads at half three in the morning was one thing but hurtling through central London at half four in the morning was altogether different. In the end it was decided that Bruce would go on a scouting mission and see if he could find something suitable in reasonable proximity to the bridge.

Bruce's first port of call was the Midland Mart estate agency in Thame where he enquired about properties for sale in the area. The very first one he looked at, a four-bedroomed farmhouse just outside the village of Brill, some twenty-seven miles from the bridge, seemed to fit the bill to perfection. He spoke to the owner, said he was interested and that he'd be in touch shortly. I suggested putting the conveyancing in the hands of Brian Field, a ten per cent deposit of £550 was paid and we had vacant possession.

While all this was going on Buster and I had been keeping observations at Euston, and the mail train kept to a very rigid schedule. One slight concern was that occasionally the HVP van was of a newer, more secure model which, whilst still do-able, would take a bit longer. I asked McKenna about it and he said not to worry, on the night of the robbery the van would be of the older type. How he could possibly know this is anyone's guess but not one scrap of his information had been wrong to date so I was prepared to take his word for it.

Charlie took on the role of quartermaster. We had no idea how long we'd have to remain at the farm but thought it best to err on the side of caution. We'd need enough food for sixteen people for maybe a week. Sleeping bags, drink, cigarettes, a few packs of cards and a Monopoly set were put on the list. As regards the robbery itself, we would need a lorry and two jeeps. The lorry and one of the jeeps we bought at auction and the second jeep we stole. It was decided to paint them khaki giving them the appearance of army vehicles, a chore which I delegated to a pal. We'd need half a dozen pairs of handcuffs and three sets of walkie-talkies. All this equipment was assembled and transported to the farm. Personal equipment – clothing, coshes, masks and gloves – was left to the individual. I elected to take my Guardia Civil truncheon and my favourite balaclava. I also took a couple of pairs of gloves, similar to those worn by orchestra conductors, which I found very comfortable and non-restrictive and you can never be too careful.

We were more or less set to go now, having made all the preparations to the best of our abilities. The date was set for August 6 straight after the bank holiday week- end but Bruce, The Schoolmaster as we called him, felt that running through everything on paper and blackboard was no substitute for a full dress-rehearsal. I had mixed feelings about it. On the one hand I could see the sense in making sure everyone knew their job and where they were supposed to be. All the crucial roles had been made interchangeable to an extent – in the robbery business you never knew if one of the team may be indisposed, nicked or for some other reason unavailable on the night. For the one absolutely critical role – stopping the train – we had no substitute. We'd just have to take it on trust that Roger would be there and knew what he was doing as regards the stopping. My reservation was that if fifteen of London's best known villains were spotted in each other's company lurking around a station doubts could be raised.

The consensus was that a rehearsal, albeit a fairly low-profile one, was the wisest option. The location chosen was Nine Elms station in Battersea. We ran through the whole routine with the exception of actually stopping the train. Everything went like clockwork, everyone knew their roles and positions, the walkie-talkies worked perfectly and we were all brimming with confidence that we were more than capable of pulling this thing off.

6

The Train

I SPENT THE August bank holiday weekend in Ireland making a futile attempt to establish an alibi. One of the family wanted no part so that was that, all or none. When I arrived back in England on August 6, Brian Field picked me up at Swindon station with some frustrating news. Paddy McKenna had been in touch and advised postponing the job until the following night. Something to do with the Wakes Week holiday in Northern England was the cause of the delay but it did mean we could expect a bumper crop. Armed with a bottle of Jameson's we set off for Leatherslade Farm to break the news.

I was the last to arrive, the others having dribbled in two or three at a time over the course of the afternoon. The delay was accepted pretty philosophically and out came packs of cards, Monopoly and a few bottles of booze. I sat with the bottle of Jameson's mulling things over with Bruce, but we'd been over it so many times there was nothing left to discuss. All were present and correct, everyone knew their job and it was just a matter of going out and getting the work done.

The next day, August 7, seemed interminable. Waiting is always the worst part and the twenty-four-hour delay had put us all a bit on edge. Finally, midnight dragged itself around and it was time to get dressed and ready to leave.

I wore jeans and a jumper, and was carrying my trusty Guardia Civil truncheon and a balaclava to be donned at the appropriate moment. Some of the lads had acquired army fatigues to continue the illusion of an army unit on manoeuvres and were all carrying an assortment of equipment – crowbars, sledgehammers, pickaxe handles and a variety of coshes. Buster and Charlie were wearing rail-workers' overalls and caps liberated from a shed by the rail-line. Bruce was wearing a paratrooper's smock and a beret with an SAS emblem affixed. I can't say for sure if there were officer's insignia attached but I'd be surprised if there weren't. The fifteen of us, plus Pops, Biggsy's train driver, climbed aboard the two jeeps and the lorry and off we headed for the bridge.

We knew the train had left Glasgow on schedule at ten to seven pulling five coaches. Four coaches were added at Carstairs and another three at Carlisle. After stops at Preston and Warrington it pulled into Crewe at half twelve. This was where driver Jack Mills took over the reins accompanied by his fireman, David Whitby. At Tamworth two more sorters joined the HVP coach which left Rugby as its last stop before its unscheduled stop at Sears Crossing.

The locomotive, D326, had a fairly chequered career. On Boxing Day, '62, it had run into the rear of the Liverpool to Birmingham express killing eighteen people and injuring another thirty-four. A year after the robbery a mechanic was electrocuted whilst working on the engine and in '66 it suffered brake failure and ran into a freight train at Birmingham New Street station causing the guard to be injured. It would eventually be withdrawn from service in '84 and scrapped to avoid the ravages of souvenir-hunters.

The Train

IT WAS A lovely, balmy summer's night as we lay sprawled on the embankment awaiting the arrival of the train. Bruce, Roy James and John Daly had been off cutting the local phone lines and were now testing the walkie-talkies. They worked fine. Roger Cordrey was up in the signal gantry waiting for Bruce's call to tell him the train was coming and to change the signal to red. His method for doing this was quite simple, if a little Heath Robinson. He had a nine-volt battery connected to a bulb by two strips of wire. This he placed behind the red lens of the signal, at the same time covering the bulb behind the green lens with a leather glove. If we'd known it was that easy we could have done it ourselves.

A couple of hundred yards before Roger's position on the gantry was a dwarf signal that had to be changed from green to amber to warn the driver that the next signal may be red. Roger had shown John Daly how to do this but John didn't make a very good job of it. Instead of covering the green bulb he simply removed it. This caused a bell to ring in the signal box to warn the signalman of a bulb failure and, had he been a conscientious chap, our window of opportunity could have been greatly reduced.

The train arrived bang on time. I suppose the thing that stuck in all our minds was Bruce's voice over the walkie-talkie: 'This is it. This is it. This is it.'

John Daly had changed the dwarf signal from green to amber and Roger extinguished the green light and switched on the red one, bringing the train to a screeching stop at Sears Crossing. The fireman, David Whitby, climbed down to walk to the phone and ring the signal box to find out what the problem was but discovered the phone lines had been cut. He was handcuffed and bundled into a ditch by Buster.

'Keep your mouth shut or you'll get hurt,' Buster told him.
'Don't worry, mate. I'm on your side,' said Whitby.

Most people, myself included, have only ever come in
close contact with a locomotive when it is stationary at
a platform. Standing on the down-slope of an embankment
and looking up, it seemed an awful long way to climb up
to the cab. I clambered up the nearside ladder whilst Buster
took the offside one and we entered the cab, or rather we
tried to. Mills, the driver, did his best to stop us. I'll give
Mills his due, in his own way he was a bit of a hero. He
fought off Buster, who couldn't get up the final steps of the
ladder with this nutter kicking out at him. But I got in the
other side, wrapped Mills in a bearhug and pulled him away,
allowing Buster to finally climb into the cab.

I handed Mills to this person who followed me up the
ladder. I have never been positive who it was because we
all had balaclavas on. This would be the point where Mills
sustained his injury. There is no doubt that he was hurt
when his head came into contact with the wall of the cab
but I remain convinced that there was nothing malicious
about it. Mills had only really made token resistance when
he realised the strength of the opposition and had done
nothing to arouse any animosity.

Roy and Jimmy White got to work uncoupling the cab
and front two coaches whilst me and Buster climbed into
the cab. Biggsy and Pops followed us up but, try as he might
Pops couldn't get the train started. Apparently when Roy
and Jimmy had uncoupled the HVP coach from the rest of
the train they hadn't known that the hydraulics had to be
re-connected to establish a vacuum before the train could
be moved. All this caused a fair amount of panic because

we had to get the train to where it could be unloaded and to get it as far away from the seventy-odd postal workers in the remaining carriage.

There was nothing for it but to coerce Jack Mills into re-establishing the vacuum and moving the train.

'Get that driver back up here,' I shouted to Buster. By this stage Mills had a handkerchief covering his head wound and was understandably very nervous.

'You are going to move this train about four hundred yards to a spot prepared for unloading,' I told him. 'Take it slowly and I will tell you when to stop.' There was no argument from Mills and after two or three minutes, which felt like two or three hours, the vacuum was re-established and the train began to inch towards the designated point.

Two poles with white linen sheeting had been staked out at the spot where the train could be unloaded. It was crucial that it was stopped at exactly the right spot or the unloading would be compromised. Even a few feet one way or the other could have made the job impracticably time consuming. Mills stopped it on a sixpence at the precise spot.

Charlie was the first into the HVP van, smashing the window and climbing through. He was followed by Tommy, Buster and myself. Jimmy Hussey, Bobby Welch, Big Alf and Frank Monroe weren't far behind.

Don't forget these postal workers were exactly that – ordinary working chaps, unaccustomed to the sort of ordeal they were facing. Of course they were frightened, probably terrified. I would have been terrified myself, put in their position. What with what appeared to be an army of giants wielding pickaxe handles, axes and coshes, it's no wonder that resistance was less than token.

The sliding doors were forced open and in less than a minute the mailbags began to rain down the embankment and were passed hand to hand onto the waiting lorry. Apparently seven bags were left behind and the reason for this is quite simply because I didn't know they were there. Had I known I most certainly would have found the extra two or three minutes it would have taken to load them. Judging by what was in the other bags we may well have left another quarter of a million sitting there – more money than I'd made on any bit of work I'd ever done before.

The forty-five-minute drive back to the farm down country roads was uneventful. The time Bruce and I had spent swotting over Ordnance Survey maps had been well spent as had the time Roy James and Jimmy White had spent rehearsing the route. Travelling west from the bridge we took C roads as far as Whitchurch, briefly joining the A413 as far as Quainton. Back to C roads to Brill and then the B4011 towards Thame, clocking a distance of twenty-eight miles. We scarcely saw another vehicle and arrived back at the farm at 4.30, just in time to hear the first reports of the robbery coming over our police scanner. I heard an excited voice come over the radio.

'You won't believe this but some bastards have only nicked a fucking train!'

Entering the lane to the farm, I recall hearing Tony Bennett on the radio singing, appropriately enough, 'The Good Life'. At least it seemed appropriate at the time.

They had no knowledge of how much had been stolen at this point but then again, neither had we. Just unloading it was a mammoth task and soon there were mail-bags everywhere – in the lounge, in the hall, up the stairs, everywhere.

Bruce went off to bed, which shows something for his nerves, while the rest of us began ripping open mailbags and stacking parcels of money on the floor. My first concern was to make sure that no tracking devices had been implanted in the bags – wouldn't do to have a posse of Old Bill beating the door down in mid-count. It would take us twenty-four hours to count the haul and we eventually arrived at the figure of two million, six hundred grand.

I've read that there was a party atmosphere. Well, if you can call counting money a party we were having a party because that's what most of the lads spent the next twenty-four hours doing. Bruce went for a kip and I spent the night at the upstairs window keeping my ears on the shortwave radio. All the talk about people lighting cigars with five pound notes didn't happen either, nor was there a game of Monopoly played with real money. We did have a few celebratory drinks right enough and, needless to say, we were all feeling very pleased with ourselves. Two point six million is a long way from the six million we'd anticipated but it would be a bit churlish to start grumbling. A hundred and fifty grand apiece was a colossal touch back in the days when you could buy a new Mini for four hundred quid. Some of the notes were Scottish, which we divided equally amongst us, and some were a bit more tatty than others but it was all spendable and practically all untraceable.

The first disquieting news was a report that a hitch-hiker, an off-duty soldier or airman, had told the police that he had seen a convoy of a lorry and a couple of jeeps heading in the direction of the bridge half an hour before the robbery. It's very likely this was a total fabrication dreamt up by the Old Bill in an effort to make us panic. If so, it had a certain amount of success. I'm a pretty observant person and I never saw any hitch-hiker and to the best of my knowledge neither did any of the others. We knew that both the previous owner of the farm and our next door neighbour had seen at least the lorry and maybe the jeeps as well. The first TV reports spoke of the police setting up a cordon of thirty mile radius from the bridge and searching isolated buildings. Actually this was slightly inaccurate. What the police had said was the cordon would be within a half-hour drive of the scene, based on a remark by one of the robbers telling the postal workers not to move for half an hour. In fact we were more like an hour's drive from the scene and well outside the cordon but we didn't know that at the time.

I tried to put things in perspective. On the face of it a thirty mile radius does sound a bit too close for comfort but let's think about it. If my old maths teacher had it right the area of a circle is pi×r². That gives us 30×30×3.142 or about 2,825 square miles. An area consisting almost entirely of isolated farms and outbuildings. Needles and haystacks was how I summed it up.

Consistent with normal practice the matter was settled by consensus and the consensus was that we should leave the farm as quickly as was reasonably practicable.

We'd all made our own arrangements about transport from the farm, most thinking the lorry and jeeps would serve the purpose but now that they appeared to be compromised other plans had to be made. Jimmy White made a half-hearted attempt to disguise the lorry using some yellow paint he'd found in a shed but it wasn't very convincing. I was to be picked up by Brian Field and taking his, mine and McKenna's shares, we'd head for Brian's house in Swindon. This now had to be revised because of the urgency and because the vehicles couldn't be used. Roger Cordrey left by bicycle for Oxford to phone Brian and get him down earlier for me. When he arrived he agreed to take Roy James back to London to arrange transport for the others and then come back for me. I dare say this was much more involvement than Brian had anticipated having but in the robbery business you have to be adaptable.

It was only as we were leaving that Buster noticed that the money had been divided into eighteen shares whereas, including Brian Field's and Paddy's, there should have been only seventeen.

'Who's the eighteenth share for?' he asked no-one in particular.

'Pops, the train driver,' chirped up Biggsy.

'Yeah? Bollocks!' I said. 'Leaving aside the fact he couldn't drive the fucking thing, he was only ever on a drink. I'm not altogether sure you're entitled to a share yourself.'

Pops got his drink and the rest of the eighteenth share was redistributed.

I stayed at Kabri, Brian's house, on the Friday and Saturday nights and then left to stash my share of the haul. Paddy McKenna arrived in a van with a false bottom in it, put his share into the hidden compartment and then drove off. I would never see him again and I wouldn't see Brian until we were in the dock at Aylesbury. The money I buried under concrete in the scullery of a property owned by me but not in my name. Sort of belt and braces if you will, I then tiled over the finished result to make doubly sure.

A friend of mine, Charlie Alexander, owned The Windmill pub in Blackfriars where I kept a room on a semi-permanent basis and where I kept a change of clothes. That seemed a suitable location to sit out the hue and cry and off I went.

7

Hunted

WE HAD ALL expected a fair amount of heat, but I don't think any of us imagined quite how hot it was going to get. We were in all the headlines, the main item on all the news bulletins and the sole topic of conversation on everyone's lips. I think it's fair to say that the opinion of the general public fell somewhere between grudging respect and outright hero-worship. The one piece of ammunition for our detractors was the injury to Jack Mills, the train driver. Without wishing to be offensive to Mr Mills's memory I think there's something worth saying at this point. There's absolutely no doubt that he played his injury to the hilt. And who could blame him? In his position I'd have done exactly the same thing. The post office was offering a reward of two hundred and fifty grand for information leading to the arrest of the robbers and/or the recovery of the money. In the meantime they'd awarded a paltry two hundred and fifty quid to Mills for doing his utmost to thwart the robbery.

During the transfer of the bags from the train to the lorry I took a quick smoke break and wandered over to where Charlie was watching over Mills and the fireman. Charlie was chatting to them and doing his best to put them at their ease. I heard Mills say 'You blokes have treated us like gentlemen.' Charlie offered to leave them a few quid, tucked under a bush but Mills declined.

In an interview a couple of days later he repeated the remark as to how the robbers were gentlemen. This was followed by an interview given by Richard Beeching, the then chairman of the British Railways Board, who said something to the effect that the robbers weren't gentlemen, they were thieving scum. Obviously Mills was ordered to toe the official line. I believe the fact that Mills never identified any of the robbers proves he had no more animosity to us than we had for him. I'm six foot four and was in his company briefly when I entered the cab with Buster. Had he chosen to, I'm sure he could have made at the very least a tentative identification of me.

The police investigation got off to a pretty rocky start. Before the photograph and fingerprint mob arrived the locomotive itself was en route back to Crewe so was unavailable for examination. For God's sake, it was a fucking crime scene! Little wonder that not one scrap of forensic evidence tied any of the robbers to the robbery site.

One disquieting development was that the investigation was being taken over by the Flying Squad under the command of Tommy Butler, who was known by some as 'The Thief Taker' and others as 'One Day Tommy' because of the speed with which he effected arrests. Apparently Butler had been appointed on the direct instructions of the Home Secretary. Detective Superintendent Fewtrell, head of Buckinghamshire CID, was left with responsibility for paperwork and exhibits, leaving Butler free to concentrate on nicking us. His right-hand man was Frank Williams, who had a better knowledge of the London underworld than any other copper on the force and they were given the entire squad and every facility to track us down. Butler was convinced from the start that his most likely route of making arrests would come from word on the street. The plan was to put so much pressure on known villains that eventually some information would come to light. It's a fact that of the first thirty or forty names to come up, most of the actual robbers were included.

This team was one we knew only too well and we knew we were being pursued by the absolute cream of the cream of British Old Bill. We knew myself, Bruce, Charlie and Buster would be right at the top of the Old Bill's target list, bearing in mind the so recent airport job. Time to make ourselves scarce.

The first person to be arrested was Roger Cordrey which came as a shock to me because, with the possible exceptions of Bruce and myself, he was the most careful and professional of the lot of us. He had made arrangements with a crooked bank manager to launder his share of the money but the screams were so loud after the robbery the bank manager was too frightened to get involved. As a temporary measure Roger paid three months' advance rent on a flat in Bourne-mouth with used ten bob notes, which had raised suspicions with the landlady, who was the widow of a policeman, and she informed the police. When he was questioned his share of the haul was discovered in his car. The man arrested with him, Bill Boal, was a total mystery to me. I'd never heard of him and he certainly played no part in the robbery. I presumed he'd merely been caught in the crossfire and would no doubt be released imminently. I was wrong. Bill, a totally innocent man, would be fitted up by the Flying Squad and eventually die in prison.

From a personal, and I suppose a slightly selfish, viewpoint Roger's arrest gave our mob a bit of breathing space. The Flying Squad had no reason to believe the two gangs had ever worked together but they did know who Roger's associates were. They would now be concentrating their efforts on the likes of Tommy Wisbey, Bobby Welch and Jimmy Hussey.

At lunchtime on Tuesday, August 13, Bruce, Buster, Charlie and Jimmy Hussey had a meeting at a café bar and Charlie popped out to buy a newspaper. He looked a bit grim when he returned. Throwing the newspaper on the table, he declared, 'Better make ourselves scarce or we're all fucking nicked.'

The discovery of the Leatherslade Farm hideout was a body blow. I wasn't concerned about any evidence I might have left behind, being certain I'd worn my silk conductor's gloves from the time I arrived till the time I left. I wasn't so certain everyone else had been so punctilious. According to the newspaper reports the police had found a 'wealth of evidence' at the farm, including fingerprints, mailbags, money wrappers and the jeeps and lorry. How all this evidence had been allowed to remain at the farm is a mystery to me. Mark, Brian Field's pal, who had come on the second meet with Paddy McKenna and whom I'd never had any time for, had been paid £28,000 to clean the place up. This was a massive amount of money bearing in mind the whole place, farmhouse, outbuilding and garage cost only five and a half grand and of that we only paid a ten per cent deposit. If we'd known it wasn't being done, as a last resort we could have burnt the place down.

More worrying still was the fact that Brian Field's boss, John Wheater, had done the conveyancing – all the more reason it was in his own best interest to ensure the place was cleaned. If he cracked we all had a problem and whilst Brian had a massive amount of experience dealing with the police he had never been interviewed in the role of suspect. Even if he didn't crack, the mere fact he had represented Buster and me numerous times would go a long way to confirming police suspicions of our involvement.

As it turned out Butler's and Williams's first port of call after the discovery of the farm was Wheater's office and they immediately smelled something fishy. The purchase price of the farm was five and a half grand but Wheater had got the vendor to agree to granting vacant possession on payment of a £550 deposit. This was explained by a claim that the place was in need of total refurbishment and the buyer wanted to get started as soon as possible. More suspicion arose when it was discovered that Brian Field had accompanied the purchaser on his inspection visit, which wouldn't be normal procedure. Then it transpired that the buyer hadn't signed the sale contract – John Wheater had. Add on Brian Field's ongoing relationship with Buster and myself and it's not surprising the Old Bill decided to put the solicitor under the microscope.

Another damning link to the farm was that when Bruce and Roy first went to view it they spoke directly to the owner. Also, on another occasion, a neighbouring farmer had called around asking if an existing arrangement for him to rent a field could be continued and Bruce had spoken to him as well. If it could be established that Bruce had been at the farm then the Old Bill would be prepared to bet their bollocks that I, Buster and Charlie had been there.

Worries about Brian's reliability became more pronounced on August 16. A couple out walking in Dorking Woods came across three bags containing a total of just over a hundred grand and reported their find to the police. Besides the money there was a receipt from a hotel in Germany made out to Mr and Mrs Field. I later learned that the money had been abandoned by Brian's father who had been minding it but panicked because of all the publicity. The money and the receipt was sent to Aylesbury police who were already aware that Field had handled the conveyancing of the farm. They went to Oxfordshire to interview him and he freely admitted having been to the hotel in Germany but denied any knowledge of the money. He also denied handling the sale of the farm saying that it was done by his boss, John Wheater. He gave a story that implicated Lennie Field, the nominal owner of the farm, who he claimed had bought it on behalf of his brother for whom Brian had acted in the past. He admitted having visited the farm once in the company of Lennie. It would be a month later before the arrests were made. Lennie was arrested on September 14, Brian on September 16 and his boss, John Wheater, two days later.

A fortnight after the robbery I picked up a newspaper to see Bruce's photo staring back at me with the caption 'Train suspects named.' Now it really was time to make myself scarce, London certainly wasn't the place to be. One particular article in the *Daily Mail* was especially disquieting, mentioning that the police had their suspicions that the same people might be involved that had been involved in the airport robbery.

The night before, I was having a drink in The Chelsea Potter when a very aggrieved Terry Hogan put in an appearance saying he'd spent a very uncomfortable few hours being grilled by the Flying Squad. They seemed to be under the impression he knew something about the robbery.

'What do you expect, Tel?' I asked him. 'You can't be a robber one day and not the next. How the fuck are the Old Bill supposed to know you've retired from the job?' It had only been a few weeks earlier, in The King's Head in Putney, that Bruce and I had asked Terry if he was interested in coming on a major piece of work and he'd refused. He repeated that he hadn't the feel for it any more and had thought they'd have got more out of the airport job. Besides which he was concerned about the amount of people involved and that they came from two separate firms. If one person broke down under inter-rogation everyone would finish up in the nick. He was going to try his hand at straight business.

Fortunately enough for Terry this gave him an inkling there was something afoot and, possibly having had his card marked by Bruce as to the approximate date, had driven to Cannes for the week covering the robbery. Years later his daughter recalled him running along the beach at Cannes the morning after the robbery waving a newspaper and shouting 'They've done it. They've done it.'

Still, it confirmed that the people from the airport job were suspected of an involvement. I had a girlfriend up in Leicester and I thought that might be an out-of-the-way enough place to spend a few weeks until the dust settled. I borrowed Charlie Alexander's car and booked a hotel room under his name and headed off. The car broke down on the way and I had to be towed to a garage but the mechanic gave me a lift into Leicester.

Unfortunately I chose to wear a pair of horn-rimmed glasses and one of the wanted pictures of Bruce had him wearing a similar pair. The girl I was meeting had won the Miss Leicester beauty contest the year before so was something of a local celebrity, which might be why the hotel staff took more notice of us than would otherwise have been the case. The hotel receptionist, having seen Bruce's picture in the evening paper, mistook me for him and phoned the police. I was rudely awakened in the early morning by two Leicester detectives accompanied by Peter Vibart, Butler's second in command at the Flying Squad.

'What's your name?' I was asked.

'Charles Alexander,' I replied.

'No it's not. He's at his pub in London. We've phoned him,' said one of them.

'He's fucking not. He's here' I insisted.

They were having none of it and off we set for Leicester police headquarters. Initially I was left in an office with a young constable and my personal possessions were left lying on the desk. I idly picked up my address book and began flicking through it. When I got to Charlie Wilson's name I snatched up a ballpoint and thoroughly deleted it.

'What the hell are you doing?' screamed the cozzer.

'It's okay mate,' I told him. 'It's just my girlfriend's number. She's married, you know.'

Before long we left for Aylesbury where I was initially interviewed by Detective Superintendent Malcolm Fewtrell, the head of Buckinghamshire CID. I frankly admitted that in fact my name was Gordon Goody and I had given a false name because I knew quite well that the police wanted to interview me over the train robbery – an event that I knew absolutely nothing about.

Fewtrell was a gentleman who came from a family with a long tradition of police service going back as far as the Bow Street Runners, but running a country force he was a bit out of his depth with the train investigation. Running two incident rooms, one in Aylesbury and the other at Scotland Yard, meant that few if any of the myriad police involved had a complete overview of the inquiry's progress. There was also a great amount of inter-force rivalry with the London police determined not to allow the country bumpkins a share of any glory.

Before long Tommy Butler arrived, who was well aware I wasn't Bruce but was none the less delighted to have the opportunity to interview me. I continued to deny all knowledge of the robbery while being as vague as possible about my whereabouts at the time. Not having found my fingerprints at the farm and having no other evidence against me, they were left as I saw it, with no choice but to let me go. Just a matter of sitting it out.

Over the next thirty-six hours I went through a few more interviews but we seemed to be going around in circles. I knew that according to section 38(2) of the Magistrates' Courts Act 1952 if the police couldn't complete their inquiries or charge me they were obliged to release me on police bail.

Butler left the room and when he returned said 'Come on Gordon. We'll give you a lift home.'

I didn't fancy this one little bit, knowing Butler and Vibart's pedigree for fitting people up. God alone knows what admissions they'd claim I'd made on the trip home. They gave me a bail form telling me I was being released on my own recognizance of a hundred quid. The form, which was dated and timed, I stuck in my sock. Surely they couldn't maintain I'd grassed myself up after I'd been given bail. As it turned out they dropped me at the end of my mother's street and the trip passed off without incident.

I'd phoned Pat, my friend who ran the hairdressing salons I owned, and she'd driven down to Aylesbury to see if she could render any assistance but by the time she arrived I'd left for London. We must have passed each other on the way. She thought saying I'd been released was some kind of ruse to keep me incommunicado and kicked up havoc. She eventually accepted I'd gone and we met the following day in London where all the reporters surrounding my mother's house were making my life a misery.

Quite honestly I felt very embarrassed about this turn of events. There were people falling all around me and here was me, one of the principals, released on a hundred quid bail. I know the thoughts that would be going through my mind if the boot was on the other foot. I felt so bad that I went to visit Charlie Wilson who by this time was on remand. He told me not to be ridiculous, he'd never have any doubts about me.

I WASN'T VERY concerned when the police got a warrant to search The Windmill pub because I knew there was nothing there that could connect me to the robbery. Amongst other things, the police took away my change of clothes that included a pair of brown suede shoes which as far as I can remember were unworn.

A few days later, on October 3 when I reported for bail, Tommy Butler was waiting to interview me.

'Are these your shoes?' he asked.

'Don't know,' I said. 'Give me a look.'

'No need for that. You're nicked,' he told me.

The shoes were wrapped in paper and I never did get a chance to examine them. Let's have it right. The lads were seriously contemplating returning to the farm and destroying any possible remaining evidence. All I had to do was pop around to my local boozer and have a clear-out, which I would have done had there been anything to clear out but there wasn't.

I was re-arrested, charged with robbery and conspiracy to rob, my bail was revoked and I was placed on remand. The police would claim at my trial that paint samples that tied me to the farm were found on the soles of the shoes.

Charlie Wilson had been arrested on August 22 after his prints were discovered at the farm. For the same reason Biggsy was arrested on September 4, Jimmy Hussey on the 7th, Tommy Wisbey on the 11th, Bobby Welch on October 25. John Daly followed on December 4 and Roy James on December 10.

The hunt was still on for Buster, Bruce and Jimmy White and to say they had to keep out of the way would be a gross understatement. The loss adjusters, Hart & Co of the City of London, had offered a quarter of a million for information leading to the arrest of the fugitives and the recovery of the money. That was nearly double the share any of the robbers had received and certainly more than enough to get all the grasses in London putting their thinking caps on. Apparently phone lines at Hart & Co were constantly engaged and daily queues were forming down the stairs and around the block with people eager to get in their claims for a share of the reward. Bearing all this in mind the dark side of the moon and further afield might be suitable hiding places for Bruce, Buster and Jimmy.

Although the police could justifiably claim a remarkable amount of success in making the arrests, their biggest embarrassment was their failure to recover much of the money. Other than the share of Roger Cordrey captured in Bournemouth the only money recovered was the money found in Dorking Woods. Then the controversy of the cash in the phone box arose.

An anonymous phone call to Scotland Yard had said that a mailbag full of money would be left in a phone box in Great Dover Street. Or at least that was how the story went. Butler and Williams had a suspect whom they had interviewed several times but due to lack of evidence had been unable to charge him. A deal was struck whereby in exchange for returning part of his whack, the line of investigation would not be pursued and there would be no fit-ups. Whether the figure was fifty grand or seventy grand and whether it was in one mailbag or two will never really be known because there were totally conflicting reports of the whole incident. At the very least Butler and Williams were guilty of fairly serious breaches of procedure in going to the phone box alone and returning with the money in Butler's car. The figure turned over to Malcolm Fewtrell at Aylesbury was £50,000 and the suspect was never charged.

8

Trial by Jury

THE COMMITTAL PROCEDURE went pretty much how committal procedures always go. All the prosecution has to do is prove to a magistrate that there is prima facie evidence that the accused have a case to answer. They are not obliged to present every scrap of evidence they have and the defence has no obligation to challenge anything at this point, though they may well do so if there is any chance of nipping the charges in the bud. The only real surprise was the appearance of Billy Boal. It was the first time I'd set eyes on him and Buster and Charlie had never seen him before either. Even amongst the South London firm the only person who had any knowledge of him was Roger who said he knew him but was fucked if he knew why he was in the dock. Seemingly microscopic samples of yellow paint similar to paint found at the farm had been discovered on the knurled winder of Boal's watch though to my certain knowledge he had never set foot on the farm. However, he was committed along with the rest of us.

We were all remanded to Bedford prison and the trial date was set for 20 January 1964 at Aylesbury Assizes. We weren't happy about that, having hoped that the trial would be moved to The Bailey, where we would have had a much better chance of jury nobbling. The court room at

Aylesbury was considered too small to accommodate all the defendants, their numerous legal teams and the droves of reporters and spectators anticipated. Instead the chambers of Aylesbury Rural District Council were adapted to house the trial and we would be ferried there each morning. The trial would be presided over by Mr Justice Edmund Davies which was a bit disquieting since he was very much an Establishment figure and the robbery was being put down as a blatant slap in the face to the Establishment. Still, nothing we could do about that; very strong grounds have to exist to have any success in objecting to a judge.

There was one amazing event whilst I was on remand. My pet dog, Sheena, had been in the car with me when I was arrested at the police station. My mother picked her up and took her home but she had been refusing to eat ever since and was in a very frail condition. My mother contacted the Home Office, an establishment not known for its compassion, and somehow got permission to bring the dog into Bedford prison on a visit. I don't think it has ever been done before or since. She never recovered and died a few days later and my mother had her buried below my bedroom window. It may sound something very trivial but it meant a lot to me at the time.

As ANYONE WHO watched the O.J. Simpson trial knows, they are nothing like *Perry Mason* or *Law and Order* – all gripping stuff from start to finish. Trials are extremely boring and jurors spend an awful long time staring about and twiddling their thumbs and no doubt a lot of their time is passed by studying the men in the dock. I think this is where we made a crucial mistake. The jury consisted of rural types, farmers and such-like, and I think that's how we should have dressed. Instead we dressed as we would have done for a night out in London and looked, well.... I suppose like a gang of criminals who got their living robbing trains.

The main thrust of the prosecution's case was that the mailbags found at the farm proved that the farm had been the hideout for the robbers so the fingerprints found at the farm belonged to the people who had robbed the train. There has been talk that the fingerprints were planted and there are people alive today that still insist that was the case. I don't know if the Old Bill had the technology back in 1963 to plant fingerprints, in fact I don't know if they have the technology today, but there was something suspect about the whole business. Apart from Tommy Wisbey's print on the towel rail – and Tommy never denied being at the farm – all the prints were found on movable objects which could have been planted. If the robbers were careless enough to leave their prints on things like a ketchup bottle, how come they never left any on the bank wrappers or any structural parts of the farm?

The farm buildings, with the mailbags, the fingerprints, the jeeps and the lorry should have been burned to the ground, as the man Mark had been paid £28,000 to do. It didn't happen so there we all were.

On February 11 we had the first inkling that the tide could be turning in our direction. John Daly was acquitted. The fingerprint expert testified that John's print had been found on a Monopoly board.

Mr. William Raeburn QC acting for Daly jumped to his feet saying 'Your honour, certainly my client plays Monopoly. In fact, several weeks before the robbery he was playing

Monopoly at the home of his brother-in-law Bruce Reynolds. His prints on the board, and the board being a portable item, in no way prove he was ever at Leatherslade Farm.'

Edmund Davies reluctantly agreed and John walked from court a free man.

In his book Butler's deputy Frank Williams holds Butler responsible for Daly's acquittal. Butler hadn't gained his meteoric elevation to head of the Flying Squad by sharing his glory with anyone and had always been very reticent about sharing information with his underlings. Williams claimed that had he known where Daly's prints had been found when he interviewed him he would have elicited denials from Daly that he had ever played Monopoly in his life. This would have made Daly's defence that he had played weeks earlier with Bruce unusable and quite likely John would have been convicted.

The forensic evidence against myself brings us back to the area of police evidence tampering and I blame it on my bit of bravado after the airport robbery. This time the Old Bill were going to make doubly sure of nailing my hat on.

The gist of the evidence was that yellow paint found on the sole of one ofthe shoes matched the yellow paint that had been used by Jimmy White at the farm in his attempt to alter the appearance of the lorry. Yellow paint was also found on the pedals of a jeep. Khaki paint on the sole was said to match the paint from one of the jeeps.

Dr Ian Holden of the Police Forensics Laboratory appeared as the prosecution expert. I think it's fair to say that he had an axe to grind bearing in mind the embarrassment I had caused to him and his colleagues at the laboratory after the airport trial. He was quoted as saying to a colleague,

'He (meaning me) isn't getting out of it this time.' Holden testified that the khaki paint samples were identical but the yellow samples were only 'similar'. When asked to quantify the chances of the two samples being found on another pair of shoes he said that the chances were so remote that if he was asked to find another pair, even if his life depended on it, he wouldn't even bother trying. Pretty emphatic right enough.

My expert was equally emphatic that the samples were dissimilar, however there's a massive difference between a witness that's an expert and an expert witness. Holden had spent his entire career pretty much equally divided between ferreting about in his laboratory and giving evidence. On top of that when a jury gets confused, as this mob surely were – I was confused myself – they tend to favour the expert with the most letters after his name. Holden had lots and lots of letters. Cecil Robbins BSc, Fellow of the Royal Institute of Chemists, and chief chemist at Hehner & Cox, was only in the halfpenny place in comparison but he had spent the past sixteen years doing nothing but spectrograph analysis. Spectrograph analysis was only one of numerous things that Holden spent his time doing. Robbins was adamant that the samples from the jeep and the sample from my shoe were not identical because the jeep samples had a distinct line through the spectrograph caused by a chromium content not found in the sample from the shoe. As regards the yellow paint, Robbins testified that the samples were 'not necessarily' from the same source.

All this bickering and confusion slightly misses the point. Either the evidence was planted as I claimed or it wasn't so whether it was 'similar' or 'identical' is neither here nor there.

But Edmund Davies had an answer to that in his summing up when he said, 'If the paint on the suede shoes was planted, as the defence claims, would it not be reasonable to assume identical and not similar paint would be planted? If not, what would be the point?' So by some sort of reverse logic, because the paint was only similar it wasn't planted.

The paint evidence against Billy Boal was treated even more bizarrely. Edmund Davies described it as 'a yellow herring' and attached little importance to it. Amazing since it was the only thing that connected either of us to the farm and if his was planted, as it had to be as he never set foot on the farm, it gives credence to my claims. If the police didn't do the planting Dr Ian Holden did.

I never drove any of the vehicles. If there was paint on the soles of my shoes and the pedals of the lorry, why was there none on the matting of the jeep? There wasn't, as photographic evidence proved. I didn't wear suede shoes on the robbery and if I had done so they would have been destroyed immediately afterwards. I'm a professional criminal with years of experience. It was standard operational procedure to systematically destroy all articles of clothing after a bit of work. I'm often described as being careful with money but, after just stealing a hundred and fifty grand, am I going to retain a cheap pair of suede shoes that could tie me directly to the robbery? I was on bail at the time the shoes were discovered and had ample opportunity to dispose of anything incriminating. I might be a thief but I'm not stupid.

One of the big weaknesses in my defence was the lack of much of an alibi. I had maintained that I'd been in Ireland on a watch smuggling expedition and the plan was for me to fly back under an alias on the sixth, do the robbery and a pal fly back on the seventh under my name. The twenty-four-hour delay botched all that. I did have something desperate that I thought of using if things were going really badly. As you may have gathered, a fair percentage of the work we planned never came to fruition and for all I knew the train could have turned out to be another aborted mission so I had been working on a contingency plan. Can't let the grass grow under your feet.

With two pals we'd put a bit of obo into a cigarette warehouse in Norwich and the plan was to have it on the eight but as things worked out I was otherwise engaged. The two pals had gone ahead with the work without me but I knew every detail of the coup. Where it was, the way in, the escape route and more or less the value of the haul. If I were to say 'Oh, alright. I'll tell you the truth. I couldn't have been at Bridego Bridge at half three in the morning because I was busy screwing a fag factory in Norwich at seven in the morning,' this is the kind of admission that a jury would find hard to disbelieve and eight or ten years for warehouse breaking looked a lot more attractive than whatever massive lump of bird was going to be dished out for the train. In the end things didn't seem to be going all that badly and I decided to stick with the watch smuggling yarn.

LET'S BE CLEAR, I'm not trying to maintain I was an innocent man fitted up. I was a guilty man fitted up doing his utmost to get unfitted up. Bill Boal was a different kettle of fish. He was an innocent man fitted up and the paint on the watch winder got there in exactly the same way as the paint on the shoes got there. It was put there.

Of course questioning police integrity put me in a very awkward position and it was a dilemma with which I wrestled. If I used this defence I was opening the door for my previous record to be read to the jury but if I didn't how would I explain the paint? In the end I decided I had little choice and thought maybe I could even use my previous to my advantage. Would an experienced, professional criminal make such a fundamental mistake in not disposing of the shoes? As things turned out the jury chose to accept the police version of events and I was found guilty.

Biggsy's case was the opposite side of the coin. A prosecution witness, a policeman I believe, let slip something about his previous convictions and he was given the option of a retrial. Probably thinking that the evidence against the rest of us would adversely affect his case he readily accepted and was later tried alone. It made little difference because he was found guilty at the subsequent trial.

Jimmy Hussey, Bobby Welch and Tommy Wisbey came up with a very elaborate explanation as to how their fingerprints came to be at the farm. A man called Ronnie Darke testified that he had been paid to deliver a lorry load of fruit and vegetables to a farm in Buckinghamshire, which coincidentally enough turned out to be Leatherslade. En route he stopped at Jimmy Hussey's place and asked him if he would follow him to bring him back. Jimmy said he was busy but Bobby and Tommy would go. During the conversation Jimmy reached in to the back of the lorry and helped himself to an apple and this was how his palm print came to be on the rear of the vehicle. When they got to the farm Tommy went upstairs to use the bathroom which is how his fingerprints came to be on the towel rail.

In the meantime Bobby, a publican by trade, spotted some firkins of ale the like of which he'd never seen before and picked one up to look at it out of professional interest. That's how his prints came to be on it. Another coincidence was that August 7 was Ronnie's birthday and he further testified that on that night Jimmy Hussey had attended his birthday party so obviously couldn't have been running around Buckinghamshire robbing trains. The problem with Ronnie's evidence was that, to the jury, he probably came across as just another Cockney spiv and we were all pissing in the same pot. At one point Edmund Davies even enquired as to why Ron himself wasn't in the dock and so little faith was put in his testimony.

When Roy James had been arrested he had twelve grand on his person but his counsel informed the court that the serial numbers proved they had been issued after the robbery and therefore couldn't be part of the proceeds. A car manufacturer was called to give evidence as to Roy's driving skills and character. He was followed by a taxi driver, Del Brown, who said he knew Roy well and had picked him up during the evening of August 7 and dropped him at a night club. He returned for him at two thirty and took him home where they sat and drank coffee until about four am. So, obviously Roy couldn't have been running around Buckinghamshire robbing trains either. The fact that Del had visited Roy a couple of dozen times whilst Roy was on remand might have led to suspicions that they had concocted the alibi.

Charlie Wilson never gave evidence. In fact he never said a word throughout the trial and for that reason was referred to as 'The Quiet Man' by the newspapers. His fingerprints were found on a couple of items that were equally as portable as the Monopoly board and the lorry so didn't prove conclusively that he had been at the farm. He must have felt he had little that had to be denied.

There comes a time in a trial, generally during the summing up, where you're either bristling with optimism or you've philosophically accepted that your goose is cooked. We were, to a man, leaning much more towards the goose than the optimism. It came as little surprise when the jury came back with guilties all round and we were remanded for sentence and sent back to Aylesbury.

The trial had lasted a total of ten weeks and more than 250 witnesses had been heard. Mr Justice Edmund Davies used two and a half million words in his thirty-three hours of summing up and the all-male jury spent sixty-six hours reaching their guilty verdicts.

In 1964, Malcolm Fewtrell, the Buckinghamshire CID boss at the time of the robbery, wrote a book, *The Train Robbers*, pointedly omitting the word great. In the book he was quite flattering to me describing me as one of the 'most fascinating characters' of the people to eventually stand trial. He said he was convinced that I was one of the leaders and that he was sure I had played a major role in the robbery but yet he would take no part in my later fit-up. In fact he told my QC, Wilfred Fordham, that 'it wasn't right what they done to Mr Goody', referring to the planted paint evidence.

9

Sentence

WE HAD ALL been kept on remand awaiting the outcome of Biggsy's retrial and on 15 April 1964 the sentences were handed down. Mr Justice Edmund Davies began by saying that this was a grave crime that warranted a grave sentence and to treat the defendants with any leniency would be positively evil. He said to put away any feeling of derring-do, it was a crime of sordid violence and was inspired by nothing more than pure greed.

I was gaoled for twenty-five years for conspiracy to rob and thirty years concurrent for armed robbery. Davies was quite flattering to me when passing sentence. He described me as the saddest case of all, a man of intelligence and with powers of leadership. He went on to say I was the type of man that, in times of war, might well go on to be awarded medals. He then qualified all that by saying that I was also a menace to society. Despite his kind words I now faced, even with full remission, spending the next twenty years behind bars. After sentencing Davies spoke privately to my QC, Wilfred Fordham, with whom he was quite friendly, and he asked that he be kept informed of my progress.

We weren't unaware of the consequences going up against the Queen and stealing the Royal Mail. Fifty years earlier it would have been a topping offence but even though we had steeled ourselves for exemplary sentences I'd be lying if I said I wasn't shocked by them. The par for the course in those days for robbery, even very serious robbery, was fifteen to eighteen years. We had all accepted we would get more but I think twenty to twenty-two was about as far as our imagination took us. However, we were professional thieves and our only option was to take it like men.

Charlie Wilson, Tommy Wisbey, Bobby Welch, Jimmy Hussey, Roy James and Ronnie Biggs received like terms.

When Jimmy Hussey was sentenced he replied, sarcastically I presume, 'Thank you very much, m'Lord.'

Roger Cordrey received twenty years for conspiracy to rob and various concurrent sentences for handling the proceeds.

Brian Field got twenty-five years with five years concurrent for obstructing justice. Lennie Field the same.

John Wheater, Brian Field's solicitor boss, got three years.

Billy Boal, the innocent man, received twenty-four years for the robbery with concurrent sentences for handling the proceeds.

I think it's fair to say the general feeling throughout Britain was that the sentences were harsh in the extreme. The previous year Davies had sat at the Appeal Court and heard the appeal of Charles Connelly. He was convicted of an armed robbery in Mitcham, Surrey in which the van driver had been shot dead. Davies had reduced his sentence from fifteen years to ten saying the original sentence had been 'excessive'. How does he equate his two decisions? I'd love to know.

ON 13 JULY 1964, Brian and Lennie Field, who were not related, won their appeals against the conspiracy to rob charges and were left with only having to serve the five-year sentences for obstructing the course of justice. The only part Lennie had played was allowing Brian to put the deeds to Leatherslade Farm in his name.

The following day, Roger Cordrey won his appeal on the conspiracy to rob charge. His fingerprints had not been found at the farm and he was now faced with only serving the handling sentences.

And on the same day Billy Boal won his appeal against the conspiracy to rob charge. The appeal judge, Mr Justice Fenton Atkinson, said, 'Given your age (he was fifty-one) and your demeanour I find it impossible to believe you were on the train.'

That being the case, if he wasn't on the train then he wasn't at the farm – only the robbery team was at the farm – so how did the paint get on the winder? There's only one possible answer. In any case he had still to serve the sentences on the handling charges, effectively fourteen years. He died in prison in 1970, convicted solely because he knew one of the robbers.

Bill Boal's successful appeal gave me grounds for optimism. If the police had planted the paint once, as the appeal judge had indirectly accepted they had, they could quite likely have planted it twice. But it was not to be, the appeal was dismissed and the sentence upheld. I can't help thinking that nowadays it would be a different story. Not just mine but every single conviction was on the basis of forensic evidence and once one piece of evidence is discredited the whole case is contaminated. I believe that in the same circumstances today we would all walk.

It may sound unbelievable that I bear no grudge against the Old Bill for the fit-up, but I don't. They were only doing the same thing I had done myself on numerous occasions. I do feel a bit aggrieved with the judiciary upholding the conviction. There was no identification, no money was found, I'd made no admissions and I had an alibi of sorts. The one piece of evidence was the paint and in light of Bill's success the paint evidence had to be at least questionable. To this day I'm still mystified as to why the paint in Boal's case was 'a yellow herring' whilst in my case it was totally damning evidence.

I stayed in close touch with Wilfred Fordham and he made several representations to the Home Office on my behalf but without success. His wife, Peta, was the first person to write a book on the robbery.

None of the other appeals were successful either and none of the other sentences were reduced. We were all refused leave to appeal to the House of Lords.

THE HUNT WAS still very much on for Bruce, Buster and Jimmy White. Alfie Thomas appeared to have left nothing incriminating at the farm and since neither Bill Jennings's nor Frank Monroe's names had come up they hadn't either. Before long two more fugitives would be added to the list.

Charlie Wilson had elected to remain at Winson Green, Birmingham, and not to go to London for the appeals. The reason for this soon became apparent – he'd made his own arrangements for early release. Prison security back then wasn't terribly stringent and at night there was a very minimal amount of staff. The staff that were on duty tended to be elderly, semi-retired officers serving out their last few years before retirement. One of these was corrupted and, for nine grand, a master key was obtained and copied. Might not seem a lot of money but remember, these night screws were probably earning twenty quid a week so nine grand represented close to ten years' wages. Three of Charlie's pals let themselves into The Green at night, tying up the staff on duty and freeing Charlie. Apparently they simply sauntered out the main gate. There's a story, probably an urban myth that says the film shown that week was *Thirty Years of Fun* with Charlie Chaplin. The story goes on that one screw made some snide remark to Charlie, as screws are wont to do, but was snide-remarking from the other side of his face the next morning when discovering Charlie had made his excuses and left.

After a few months in hiding, he took a ferry to Calais dressed as a hitchhiker and headed to the French Riviera where he was joined by his wife, Pat. Obtaining a forged passport in the name Alloway he eventually made his way to Canada.

Biggsy's escape was altogether more dramatic. He was being held in Wandsworth and recruited a very professional team to organise his departure. A furniture van with a trapdoor cut in the roof was driven up to the south wall of the prison, next to the exercise-yard. A diversion was created and Ronnie, with his pal Eric Flower, who was serving a twelve year sentence, dashed to the wall and shimmied up a rope-ladder that had been lowered down by the awaiting team. Climbing through the trapdoor of the van, the team and the two fugitives sped away. Not long afterwards Ronnie and Eric were safely tucked away in Australia.

Ronnie wasn't very good at keeping a low profile and over a few drinks with any expatriates he bumped into he would freely admit to his true identity. On top of all that there was a world-wide hunt going on for Lord Lucan who had disappeared when wanted for questioning over the murder of his child's nanny. Whether Ronnie was caught up in the crossfire of this investigation or if it was simply lack of discretion is not known but in any case his house was raided one morning and he was only missed by a whisker.

On the trot again Ron headed for Brazil on a crooked passport and wound up in Rio. Before long Tommy Butler discovered his whereabouts and set off to make his arrest. In the meantime Ron's wife, Charmian, had returned to England and he had established a relationship with a Brazilian girl called Ramunda. Under Brazilian law a person cannot be extradited if he is the father of a male Brazilian child and it turned out Ramunda was pregnant with a male child. The extradition request was denied and Ron was allowed to remain in Rio.

A few years later he was having a drink with some British tourists and at the end of the evening he was invited back to their boat to continue the festivities. They turned out to be mercenaries who had been paid to kidnap Ron and take him to a country that had extradition with Britain. They tied him up and set sail but bad weather forced them into Barbados, or at least that's how the story goes. I have my suspicions that the whole thing was an elaborate publicity stunt to promote Biggsy's forthcoming autobiography. It transpired that the extradition treaty between Barbados and Britain had lapsed and if he knew that, and he'd certainly be in a position to discover that kind of thing, perhaps Barbados was the intended destination. In any case Biggsy escaped extradition for the second time and was returned to Rio where he was given a hero's welcome and a Brazilian passport.

Admittedly, if I'm right, it was a terrible gamble to take but what were his options? While he had the right of residence in Brazil he didn't have a work permit and was surviving mainly on the largesse of visiting tourists. Getting a photo taken with Biggsy was on every tourist's to-do list – along with the Sugarloaf, Corcovado and the Maracana Stadium – when visiting Rio and the exchange of a few quid was a given. If the autobiography was a big seller Biggsy's immediate problems would be solved. Later there was a rumour abroad that the man who financed the kidnap was the comedian Jim Davidson which, if true, goes a long way to confirming my suspicions. What possible axe could a man like Jim Davidson have to grind in seeing Biggsy back behind bars? Had the rumours been that Tommy Butler was the financier I'd be more inclined to believe that the episode was genuine.

On the other hand the leader of the kidnappers, a bloke called John Miller, had recently launched a security company and perhaps he thought recapturing Biggsy would be good publicity for this venture. I called a meeting with some of the chaps, including Bruce, Buster and Charlie, where we discussed the pros and cons of kidnapping the head kidnapper and returning him to Rio where there was, probably still is, a warrant out for his arrest, but nothing came of the scheme.

THERE WERE VERY nearly several more fugitives at large during the time we were awaiting sentence at Aylesbury. We were being held in the old hospital wing and through the offices of a bent screw I managed to get my hands on a key blank, a warding file and a wood chisel. I filed down the key blank and made a functioning skeleton key which would open my cell door. In those days the lock used universally in the British prison system was the Gibbons. This lock was notoriously easy to open and as a young prisoner I had seen old lags open them with a teaspoon. Of course nowadays that's all changed since Chubb took over the prison security. There's no question that Chubb make the best locks in the world and now I'm virtually penniless I often kick myself that I didn't buy shares in Chubb in the early days. Probably be a millionaire today. Still, it's only money. Whilst doing a bit of work with the cleaners I had discovered a staircase at the top of which was a door that gave access to the eaves. Since the eaves overhung the main street of Aylesbury, removing a few slates would give access to the roof from where a number of sheets tied together would get us down to the street.

The one snag was the lock on my cell door which could only be opened from the outside. The door had a hatch about nine by five inches that when opened stood at right angles to the door. This made it impossible to reach over and stretch down to insert the skeleton key in the lock. However, the lock on Bill Boal, Roger Cordrey and Lennie Field's dormitory cell was only a simple mortise which was where the wood chisel came in. It wouldn't take an awful lot of ingenuity for the wood surrounding the mortise to be removed and the door would open. The skeleton key could then be recovered from its stash in the toilet recess and be used toopen my door from the outside. I could then release Charlie, Tommy Wisbey, Brian Field and Jim Hussey.

The day before the planned escape the key was discovered in the recess. Biggsy was awaiting retrial, which was why we were all awaiting sentence, so was taking no part in the escape but Brian Field and Bill Boal had every reason to be optimistic of their chances at appeal. We'll never know if the key was discovered by chance or if a slightly reluctant escapee let something slip. Either way, the escape plan, unlike the key, was in the toilet.

Needless to say the two successful escapes provoked outrage and security on the rest of us was intensified. Questions were raised in Parliament and top-level inquiries launched. People in seemingly responsible positions came out with some outlandish scenarios. Thomas Muir, the chief constable of Durham, where some of us were to be held, went as far as to broach the possibility of explosives, tanks and even nuclear weapons being used in an escape attempt. Utter bollocks. He went on to suggest shooting us would be an attractive solution and even volunteered to do the job himself.

Meanwhile Bruce, Buster and Jimmy White were still at large and living in hiding. Having spent time on the trot myself I knew they would be having a pretty traumatic time of things. And expensive, with all the changing of addresses and people having their hands out every time a favour was required.

With the sentences that had been handed out Bruce was the first to decide he would have to leave England for good. Armed with a false passport that I had provided for him before the airport robbery, in the name Clemens he arranged the charter of a light plane and was smuggled over to Ostend, Belgium. False passports were remarkably easy to obtain back then. The old white twelve month-ers could be obtained with very little formality at any post office but were only good for quick continental trips. The ten year ones were a bit more difficult but presented nothing insurmountable. A good trick was to lightly brush the file photo with Billy Blue so that after a few weeks in the archives the photo would be unrecognisable. To this day I have a snide passport which has been renewed several times and is still valid, though I've never used it.

From Belgium Bruce flew to Mexico City. He had been torn between South Africa and Mexico, finally deciding on Mexico mainly because of the lack of an extradition treaty with Britain. Shortly later he was joined by his wife Frances and son Nicky and set about establishing himself as a legitimate businessman. In partnership with a Jewish-Mexican businessman he bought the franchise for Dunhill and they set about opening a factory to produce soaps and perfume under the Dunhill licence.

Buster had bought a package deal which included transportation out of Britain on a cargo boat to Germany, plastic surgery, a new passport and a Swiss bank account. All very expensive. The first operation was a failure and he had to undergo a second one but by early '65 he was ready to begin the rest of his life. He contacted Harry, knowing he would be able to get in touch with Bruce. He asked Harry to find out how Bruce would feel about him joining him in Mexico but Bruce had mixed feelings. On the one hand it would be good for the two families to have some time together but on the other hand there was the security risk of them all being spotted together. In the end Bruce told Harry to tell Buster to come on over.

No sooner were the plans made than another call from Harry informed Bruce that Charlie Wilson, who was living in Montreal, wanted to come down and pay a visit. On the sheep for a lamb principle Bruce said why not.

They had a few very pleasant weeks down in Acapulco but Charlie was far from impressed with Mexico, his biggest problem being the language. He suggested Bruce and Buster give Canada a try and invited them to Montreal.

Buster was a fish out of water in Mexico and never really settled. His wife June was a Londoner born and bred, as he was himself, and it didn't take long for the novelty of Mexico to wear off. On top of all that the money was getting smaller and smaller with no sign of any more coming in. He began making advances, through an intermediary, to the Old Bill as to what the attitude would be if he gave himself up. Would they accept a guilty plea to something like accessory after the fact? If he claimed to have only been employed as a clean-up man after the robbery could he realistically expect something like a five or a seven year sentence?

Whilst all this pondering was going on, in April '65 the news hit the papers of Jimmy White's arrest. Besides fingerprint evidence found at the farm, thirty-five grand had been discovered in the wall of a caravan owned by Jimmy, parked on a site in Suffolk. When, in June '65, Jimmy was convicted and sentenced to a comparatively lenient eighteen years Buster began to think that perhaps time had healed a few wounds and the prison terms were getting a bit closer to par for the course. He began to make plans to return home and surrender himself.

In the September Buster bit the bullet and flew back to Britain where he went to stay with a friend while he made arrangements to surrender himself. Frank Williams, Tommy Butler's number two, came personally to arrest Buster but his offer to plead guilty to being an accessory was refused and he was charged with robbery and conspiracy to rob. At Nottingham Assizes the following December he was sentenced to fifteen years. A lot more than he'd hoped for but about half of what he could have expected had he been tried two years earlier.

Bruce's time in Mexico was coming to an end, too. Cheap as Mexico was, living the lifestyle that Bruce wanted to live was more expensive than he could afford and the Dunhill venture wasn't showing the returns he expected. He took Charlie up on his offer and the Reynolds family moved up to Montreal but before long he decided to give the West Coast a visit and moved to Vancouver. Things didn't work out, what with visa problems and the lack of work opportunities, and they made plans to return to the South of France – a place where they had spent many happy times.

Charlie's time at liberty would come to an end in 1968. A friend visiting him from England was followed by the Old Bill and Charlie's hideaway was discovered. At least that's the way the story goes but the 'friend' was actually Charlie's business partner and had every reason to want to see Charlie back behind bars. This was the same chap that I had used as a getaway driver for the railway station job at Hounslow where he was waiting two streets away when the work went off. Couldn't trust him much after that. The British police got the Mounties to keep the place under surveillance for a few weeks, hoping Bruce might show up. When he didn't, Tommy Butler arrived like the avenging angel and placed Charlie under arrest. He was extradited back to England to resume his thirty year sentence.

Bruce's money was rapidly running out on the Riviera and he was left with little choice but to return to England

and try and get a bit of work done. They arrived back in early 1968, first renting an apartment in London but soon finding a more out of the way house in Torbay, Devon. Bruce went in search of Brian Field, who by this time had been released from his five year sentence. I had repeated to Bruce the remark that the Ulsterman had made to me that if the train was a success he had a bigger job we might be interested in but Brian had changed his name on his release and Bruce was unable to make contact with him.

Things were a bit hard for Bruce at this stage. Most of the people he had worked with for years were locked up and most of the others were reluctant to get in bed with him given his still very high profile fugitive status. On the other hand his ability to put a job together wasn't in doubt and he still had enough connections to get a few efforts afoot but luck seemed to be against him and nothing seemed to go right.

Whether by fluke, bad luck or from information received will never be known but the hideout in Torbay was discovered and Bruce was arrested shortly before Christmas of 1968. The evidence against him was pretty damning and rather than run the risk of his family and friends being charged as accessories Bruce agreed to plead guilty. It was also his only chance of any leniency since the papers had been reporting for years that he was one of the principals. At Aylesbury Assizes on 14 January 1969, he was sentenced to twenty-five years' imprisonment.

10

Thirty Years

With all my appeals exhausted and short of any escape opportunities arising, I was faced with having to serve at least the next twenty years behind bars. We'd been lodged at Pentonville pending the appeals and I bumped into Billy Collins, also awaiting an appeal. Billy was a keep fit fanatic and a very good welterweight amateur boxer, known as the Aldgate Tank. He was also a dyed-in-the-wool escapee. At the time he was serving fifteen years for his part in an armoured car robbery with Roy Shaw and Tony Anthony.

Walking around the yard one day we noticed that two works screws were conducting some repairs to the wall. One was working at the top of a ladder and the other was holding the ladder for him. Billy whispered that on our next circuit he was going to make a dash for the ladder. No sooner said than done, he steamed at the screw on the ground who didn't fancy himself one little bit and did his utmost to get out of the way. Billy chinned him and then proceeded to shake the other screw off and was up the ladder in a flash. How he got down the other side of the wall remains a mystery but the next thing he was flying down Pentonville Road. He must have looked pretty conspicuous since he was wearing 'patches' – a prison uniform worn by potential escape risks with a bright yellow stripe down one leg and the opposite sleeve. A passing squad car spotted him in a phone box and before long he was back inside.

Billy eventually was sent to Hull where he adopted a regime of civil disobedience. He slung all the furniture out of his cell and scrawled the words 'yes' and 'no' on the wall. Whenever a screw asked him anything he simply pointed to one or other of the words but refused to give a verbal reply. For reasons best known to himself he decided to become a Buddhist and went on some sort of religious fast. When he came off the fast he bought himself a can of peaches from the canteen and managed to choke himself to death. At least that was the story told to me by the medical officer at Parkhurst when I made enquiries after hearing of Billy's death.

The robbers were all dispersed to separate prisons the length and breadth of England. I found myself in Strangeways, Manchester, a particularly dismal hole in a system known for its dismal holes. Built in the 1860s it lacked even basic requirements, a chamber pot being the nearest you got to toilet facilities. The food was nothing short of appalling and had to be collected from a servery and eaten back in the cell. Or thrown out the window, as the mood took you.

The governor of the place was a Captain Brown who had seen service in the Tank Corps. He'd been the victim of an attack in which his tank caught fire and his face was badly scared, hence his nickname Scarface Brown. The injury had done nothing to enhance his disposition which blended quite nicely with the rest of the staff. Most screws were ex-army and few of them had risen above the rank of private so having a bit of authority for the first time in their lives they made the most of it.

On arrival I was lodged in a west-facing cell on the first floor of A Wing, the reception wing. The window gave me a clear view of the main gate and my first morning I was greeted by a particularly grizzly sight. Whilst shaving I looked out to see a middle-aged civilian and a younger bloke walk through the gates carrying holdalls. It was the hangman and his assistant en route to execute one of the last two people to be hanged in Britain. Gwynne Evans and Peter Allen had been convicted of the murder of John West, a Liverpool bookmaker on April 7 and been sentenced to death on August 13. Unlucky for some. Shortly later I saw two screws wheeling a loaded four-wheeled barrow past the window heading towards the incinerator, presumably carrying the bedding of the unfortunate Evans which by tradition is burned after the execution. Welcome to Strangeways. Peter Allen was hanged simultaneously at Walton prison, Liverpool.

After a few days I was moved to C wing. Being Category 'A' meant I was accompanied everywhere I went by two screws with a notebook logging my movements. The cell light remained on twenty-four hours a day, though admittedly at night it was a red light which was marginally less disruptive, and I was obliged to remove my clothes which were put in a cardboard box outside the cell.

I was given a job in a workshop painting toy soldiers, one of the typically menial tasks they found for prison employment. Still, better than sewing mailbags – would have been ironic getting paid to make mailbags bearing in mind I was serving thirty years for nicking a hundred and twenty of the fucking things. Workshops were silent in those days, as were most other places. The only place you were allowed to speak was on the exercise yard and even there only to the person next to you but the lack of conversation was no great hardship to me. I've always been a very private person and in any case I didn't know a soul in Manchester. Exercise was an hour a day which didn't seem enough in summer and seemed interminable in winter. The yard consisted of a series of concentric circles with alternate circles walking in the opposite directions and a couple of dozen screws with several dogs guarding the perimeter. We'd all shuffle around for the hour and that would be that until the next day.

One afternoon on the yard a bloke said to me, 'What do you think of that?'

Looking up I spotted a very colourful bird. 'What is it?' I asked. 'A parrot?'

'No,' he said. 'It's a pigeon. I caught it and painted it.'

I delivered a sharp right hook which put him on his arse, no less than he deserved. It could have cost me a week in punishment but it would have been worth it. How could he do that? Pigeons aren't my favourite bird, but still.

APART FROM FEMALE company the biggest deprivation in prison is drink. Although Irish whiskey was my normal tipple I was more than willing to make do with a drop of vodka and it didn't take me long to find a screw who, for a consideration, was prepared to smuggle me some in. I even put up with it arriving in a polythene bag. Drugs, which were readily available, were something I had little to do with though I could be talked into the odd joint of cannabis. The harder stuff, cocaine and, particularly, heroin I gave a total miss unlike a lot of the lads who saw hard drugs as a relief from the daily grind.

The panic caused by Charlie's escape saw me put on Rule 43 and I was in isolation for six months. Eventually I was returned to the general population and sent to work in the tailors shop. There was a Liverpool burglar working next to me and one day in the toilet recess he broached the subject of escape and would I be interested in taking part in one. I replied that I most certainly would and asked what he had in mind.

The workshops were in a compound adjacent to the prison and accessed via a tunnel through the main prison wall. The Scouser pointed out that the roof of the toilet was asbestos and he reckoned that over a period of time he could steal enough tools to gradually cut a series of holes. If I could arrange for a hacksaw blade to be smuggled in the holes could be joined up and we'd only have the barbed wire fence to contend with which could be cut with home-made wire cutters. We spent months drilling the holes one by one and were even at the stage where I was sorting out some getaway vehicles when disaster struck. I was dragged from the workshop and searched and then taken to my cell which was also searched, but nothing was found. I was at a loss to know what had gone wrong until the news broke that Biggsy had had it away from Wandsworth.

Because the landing light outside my cell was brighter than the night light inside, the clothes box cast a shadow beneath the door jamb. That evening I was mildly surprised to notice there was no shadow but the mystery was soon solved. The door flew open, the box of clothes was thrown at me and I was told to dress and gather my personal possessions. I was being transferred. In prison parlance this is known as being 'shanghaied' or 'ghosted'. Prison authorities feel at their most vulnerable to an escape attempt when a prisoner is in transit and for this reason a prisoner, particularly a high risk one like myself, is given no notice as to when or to where he is being moved. Can't have any associates lurking en route to effect his release.

It didn't take me long to realise we were travelling east on the A62 so my best guess was Armley Prison, Leeds but an hour later we were on the Leeds bypass and on to the A1 heading north. Now there was only one possible destination – Durham. It's hard, no not hard, impossible, to come up with a prison further from London than Durham and for this reason it was the least popular destination for a Londoner with family. A half hour visit necessitated a two day excursion for the visitors.

Visits weren't quite as big an issue for me being a single man. I'd made it clear to my girlfriend Pat at the end of the trial that there was little point in continuing our relationship since the chances of a young girl waiting twenty years or more were less than remote. Why endure the purgatory of a few years of diminishing letters and visits until the final parting arrived. Much better to make a clean break from the start. My mother and sister came to see me regularly but being on the 'A' list meant my visitors had to be approved by the Home Office. Most of my pals would have an uphill battle getting approval.

One time my mother, sister and the one pal who could get in travelled up sharing a carriage with Jimmy Savile. My mum would be turning in her grave if she heard the stories that have come out since about him. Getting off the train the newspaper people were pushing and shoving to get a photo of Savile and one got a shot of my mother in the picture which led my pal to snatch his camera and hurl it across the railway lines. The Old Bill got involved and my pal had to pay for the camera to avoid getting nicked.

Reminded me of a time at Uxbridge magistrates prior to the airport trial. As I was leaving a copper warned me the photographers were outside and suggested I leave by the back door. A photographer walked towards me with his camera around his neck but I realised he was snapping me with a remote in his pocket. I grabbed the strap and yanking the camera away I slung it down the street – must have gone twenty five or thirty yards. Bit churlish I know but I never did have any time for the paparazzi.

Amongst the rest of the gang, those with wives and children, a remarkable proportion of their marriages did survive. Buster and June were re-united until Buster's death. Tommy and Rene Wisbey stuck together despite the trauma of losing a daughter in a car crash. Charlie and Pat Wilson likewise survived the separation. Jimmy Hussey and his girlfriend Gill lost contact briefly midway through his sentence but were re-united and got married when Jimmy got parole. Bruce and Franny Reynolds were divorced for a time but had a reconciliation and remarried. Jimmy White's wife Sharee went to live in Essex where she and their son were waiting patiently for Jimmy on his release.

I had a pleasant surprise awaiting me when I arrived on the security wing where Tommy Wisbey and Roy James were waiting to greet me. Several other London faces were also on the wing. Micky Keogh, doing eighteen years for armed robbery and John McVicar, the only man to succeed in escaping from Durham, were there. So were Wally Probin, Bill Curbishley, who later managed rock groups like The

Who and Judas Priest, Albert Reddy and Gus Thatcher, all in the robbery business. Gus later became an accomplished playwright and had one of his works, *The 40 watt Light Bulb*, performed in the West End. The Moors Murderer Ian Brady was housed in the unit but he was kept well away from us. He would later be sent to Broadmoor where he remains to this day and surely will until he dies.

The company was about the only pleasant thing as regards Durham. The screws were even bigger misanthropes than their colleagues at Strangeways and seemed to reserve a particular vindictiveness for Londoners, apparently regarding us as nothing more than flash Cockney spivs.

Security at Durham E-Wing was unprecedented at a British penal institution. On the orders of Roy Jenkins a troop of fifteen soldiers and NCOs of 1st Lancashire Regiment were despatched from their base at Catterick to reinforce the prison officers. I think I'm right in saying that it has never been the case before that machine gun emplacements were constructed on a prison wall and squaddies toting Bren guns supplemented the screws supervising the exercise yard. The squaddies didn't appear to regard this duty as a cushy number and were quite vocal at voicing their discontent, often at around two in the morning.

The exercise yard in the security unit was tiny and what with the screws and their dogs and the squaddies and their guns there wasn't room to swing a cat. I went to see the Medical Officer to ask if we could be given decent exercise facilities but he said that he couldn't recommend any changes to the governor because he didn't want to hear a burst of gun fire. Before long we decided not to put up with it any longer and went on strike. For three months none of us set foot on the yard.

I spent about eighteen months at Durham until one morning in the early hours Roy, Tommy and I were shanghaied again. The three of us were bundled into three Jags and a high-speed convoy which included a couple of squad cars and a few motorcycle escorts headed for God knows where. This was the first time I'd ever seen ratchet handcuffs. Prior to this trip I'd only ever seen the old-fashioned screw cuffs — the device that gives rise to the slang name 'screw' for a prison officer. Incidentally, the screw handcuffs were remarkably easy to open using a piece of string or even a few strands of hair. Probably why they were superseded.

The good news was we were travelling south which had to be a step in the right direction and round breakfast time we found ourselves in Nottingham. Another convoy arrived bringing Jimmy Hussey and Roger Cordery. Tommy was packed off to join Bobby Welch in Leicester while Roy, Jimmy, Roger and I continued our journey south.

Lunchtime found us in Southampton where we boarded the ferry, shackled to the floor, for the trip across the Solent. By mid-afternoon we had arrived in the Special Unit at Parkhurst. These Special Units had come about as a result of The Mountbatten Report which suggested putting all the rotten eggs in one basket and we were the first to take up residence.

Parkhurst is not the easiest place to visit but certainly much more accessible from London than Durham and before long we were joined by quite a few acquaintances. Both of the Kray twins spent time there though for a long time not together. Charlie joined us in 1968. Harry Roberts, serving life for the murders of three policemen in Shepherds Bush, was another resident.

There was a fairly live–and–let–live relationship between the prisoners and the staff in the unit. Everyone was serving a long sentence and a good few had very little to lose. The facilities were much better than other places, with a tennis court, a snooker table and TV room. We had a vegetable garden where we grew our own vegetables and we were the first prisoners allowed to spend our own cash. The system used in other prisons was that purchases could only be made with prison earnings but we did very little in the way of work so had no earnings.

Prisons were much tougher places in those days. Prisoners outside the unit surviving on prison income had it very hard. A smoker, and most prisoners were in those days, could just about stretch to an eighth of an ounce of tobacco, a few papers and six matches. The norm was to split the matches into four or six splinters with a razor blade or pin giving two or three dozen lights for the week. The food was appalling and even non-smokers could only afford the odd pot of jam or marmalade. 'Civvy' soap and toothpaste were absolute luxuries and practically everyone made do with government-issue 'White Windsor' soap and tooth powder.

In modern times new arrivals are greeted with a 'welcome pack', a bit like Butlins, containing tobacco, papers, matches, biscuits, soap, toothpaste and other bits and pieces. They're given a menu card to tick off which options they'd like for lunch and dinner for the coming week. Things like radios, satellite TVs, CD players and computers are just routine accessories that anyone would expect to have. Don't get me wrong, I don't begrudge anyone these innovations. Far from it. If I was running the prison service, licensed bars and brothels would be only two of the things I'd be instigating so I merely mention all this as a comparison.

In Parkhurst the punishment block, or 'chokey' as it was known, was on the landing directly below my cell. Any breach of discipline could result in a period on punishment and a loss of all privileges — cigarettes, books, newspapers, letters and visits were all disallowed. Apparently food was also considered a privilege and a sentence often included a period, usually fifteen days, of 'restricted diet'. This was served in cycles of three days of normal diet followed by three days of bread and water — a pound of bread and 'sufficient' water every day.

It was customary for the lads above chokey to do whatever was in their power to alleviate the discomfort of their colleagues. This was done by lowering a cup attached to a length of string which might contain tea or tobacco and matches, maybe a bar of chocolate or some fruit. One night I was performing just such a mission of mercy for a pal of mine, Billy Anthony, when a passing screw spotted me and got on his radio. The next thing I knew I was in chokey myself. When I returned to my cell after punishment I found the screws, in a fit of pique, had wrecked my cell and smashed anything worth smashing.

Reggie Kray came to my cell one afternoon and told me he was being transferred to Leicester. He was under the impression he was about to join his brother Ronnie but this must have been a fanny to get him to go quietly because the next day Ronnie appeared in the unit. They must have passed each other on the motorway.

Ronnie was pretty aggrieved because he was also under the impression he was being moved to join his brother. He voiced his discontent fairly vocally to the principal officer and demanded to see the governor. Since he was under very heavy medication, which he claimed was being diluted, he also demanded to see the medical officer but was told to make an application the next morning. Sure enough, the next morning, as I was going out to empty my piss-pot, Ronnie marched past my cell en route to make his application to the landing officer who was standing on the bridge with a clipboard and pen.

'Put me down to see the governor and the MO,' he said.

'Yeah? Name?' enquired the screw.

'Fucking name? I'll give you fucking "name?" you cunt,' replied Ronnie and gave the screw a straight right to the jaw. 'FUCKING RONNIE KRAY.'

Needless to say Ronnie was jumped on by five or six screws, the 'liquid cosh' was administered and he was dragged off to chokey. After his spell on punishment he was moved to the hospital so none of us saw him for a month or so. On his return to the wing he began to tell me about this lovely bloke called Angel he'd met over in the hospital.

'Oh, Gordon. He's gorgeous. Looks just like Cliff Richard,' he said.

Apparently Ronnie was smitten and had fallen in love.

Ronnie and Reggie would eventually be re-united but it took years. I always found it difficult to work out what made Ron and Reg tick. They were both moderately good boxers and had managed to acquire a punchbag, gloves and other boxing paraphernalia with which they would train most afternoons. About once a week they would fight three two-minute rounds during which they would bash seven shades of shit out of each other. After the fight they would then become the best of pals again until the following week's bout.

When I was a kid my mother and father would occasionally, for a special treat, take me to Chelsea Palace, one of those old-time vaudeville shows. One of the acts was a stripper called Jane of the Daily Mirror whose performance would be considered very mild by today's standards. On one occasion I won 'the spotlight prize' and had to go on stage to receive a hamper and a kiss from Jane, all a bit embarrassing for a lad my age. My mother loved Irish music and one of her favourite singers was Cavan O'Connor, known as the Strolling Vagabond. She particularly like his version of 'Danny Boy' so, years later, it came as a pleasant surprise to hear that very song, sung by Joseph Locke, wafting down the landing in Parkhurst. I went to investigate and discovered it was coming from a record player in Ronnie Kray's cell. I told him of the family connection and he told me to take the record and play it.

A few weeks later I was preparing for a visit from my mother and when I returned from the showers I found an LP lying on my bed with a note attached saying 'give this to your mother'. It was a recording of Cavan O'Connor singing 'Danny Boy' which Ron had got a screw to go into town and order. What a nice gesture.

Mind you, you could catch Ron on an off day. One time I was playing snooker with Dennis Stafford when I noticed Bernie Beatie walking along the 'ones' and opening the door to Ron's cell. Next thing there was a crash and Bernie staggered out covered in what I thought was blood. I ran up to find out what was going on and discovered Ron had thrown a plastic bottle of Ribena at Bernie. Not as bad as it might have been.

'What happened?' I asked him.

'Don't know,' he said.

'He shouldn't have said that,' said Ron, joining us.

'What did he say?' I asked.

'He said, "Beautiful day out there. Not going out for a bit of exercise?"'

Sounded pretty harmless to me but you always had to be a bit careful around Ron.

Bernie was keen to learn to play the clarinet and I got my sister to go to Boosey & Hawkes in Cambridge Circle and buy him one and he did become quite proficient on it. Twenty-odd years later I walked into a bar in Mojacar and the barman placed a whiskey in front of me telling me it was from the bloke in the corner. I've always been very reluctant to get into conversation with people I don't know and it took a minute or two to realise it was Bernie.

'Still playing the clarinet?' I asked him.

He was. By this time he was living in Germany and running a successful engineering company. Small world.

Of course not all the residents of the unit were the type of people you would want to have a glass of whiskey with. Career criminals, reasonably enough, reserve a particular repugnance for rapists and especially child molesters. Probably the most pathetic person I ever came across in the unit was John Straffen. He'd been arrested for the murder of two young girls but had been found incompetent to plead and sent to Broadmoor. He hadn't been there long when they gave him a job doing a bit of yard sweeping. Placing one dustbin on top of another he managed to get himself over the wall and was on the trot for four hours and sixteen minutes. During this time at large he murdered a third child.

On this occasion he was sentenced to death but the Quaker Society got involved in his appeal and the sentence was commuted to life imprisonment. There was no doubt that he was severely retarded and probably had the mind of a ten-year-old but that didn't make his presence in the unit any more acceptable. For his own safety he spent much of his time in isolation and somehow got permission for a TV in his cell, an unheard of event back in those days. He'd sit glued to it watching programmes like *The Magic Roundabout*. He would become Britain's longest ever serving prisoner spending fifty-one years behind bars before his death in 2007.

MEDICAL TREATMENT IN prison is fairly basic and the first line of defence that has to be breached is the Medical Officer, who will always assume that any claimed illness is a fabrication in order to avoid some unpleasant task. However, to be fair, once an ailment is found to be genuine, treatment is usually forthcoming.

A few years into my sentence I began to suffer terrible back pains and before long I was walking in little pigeon steps. A few visits to the MO resulted in little more than the administration of aspirin water since complaints of back pain are always looked on as highly suspect. One morning, unable to bend over, I was trying to wash by splashing water up over my face when I collapsed. The next thing I knew was Roy James standing over me remarking how white I was. The MO was called and I was moved to the hospital wing.

A Mr Smythe of Harley Street was brought in to examine me and he diagnosed a double displacement of some discs. An operation was performed and I have been right as rain ever since.

Another time I developed a very persistent rash on my ankle. Several lotions were prescribed without much sign of improvement and eventually the civilian doctor was called in. He prescribed a new lotion, remarking, 'This'll work. It's like that gear they put in Palmolive soap – nine guineas an ounce.' The rash was gone in a few days.

THERE HAD BEEN a lot of talk on the prison grapevine on the subject of parole but very little from an official stand-point. One day Harry Roberts and I were giving our cells a bit of a spruce up with a fresh coat of paint. We heard the keys go in the main entrance and paused to see who was paying us a visit. Visiting dignitaries weren't unusual in the unit – judges, senior policemen, politicians, even had James Callaghan turn up one day. This time, amongst a posse of lawyers, was Sir Arthur James, QC, the man who had prosecuted me. I couldn't resist the urge to shout 'Happy now?'

'I beg your pardon?' he said.

'I asked if you were happy with the sentences now.'

'Ah, Mr Goody. Let me tell you that nobody had envisaged that the sentences you would receive would be so severe and all I can tell you is that there are steps afoot to put things more into perspective.'

A few days later I received a letter, without letterhead or signature, which read as follows:

WGF (Wilfred Fordham, my QC), Mr John Mathew and Mr Jeremy Hutchinson saw Sir Arthur James on Thursday and discussed in detail the probable course of events regarding all of you. The opinion they formed at the end of it is that after about 8 years, if all reports are favourable, there is a real prospect of a move to an open prison or possibly a hostel for about a year, when parole will follow. This would make a sentence in all of about 9-10 years. This, they are told, really represents the thinking of both The Home Office and the Parole Board. As you know, Sir Arthur is a member of the Parole Board as well as a judge and he has approved the passing on of this information to you, as he feels it will be an encouragement to you all to settle down and serve the remainder of your sentences, realising you have everything to gain by good behaviour. As to White and Edwards: you should not worry if their parole is granted at or about the end of one-third of their shorter sentences. If they are released at this earlier date, it will provide the opportunity for a graceful reduction in sentences without anyone losing face over it. Of course, if this were done, it would obviously advance the date of your parole. Meanwhile, we will continue to press for the earliest possible dispersal dates and are not unaware of the extra strain which you would all be subjected to if new trouble-makers are drafted into your community.

This was a huge boost to all of us since it not only confirmed all the rumours about parole but it was the first inkling that we would be live contenders to be granted it.

In 1971 I was taken off the 'A' list and transferred to Wormwood Scrubs. At last I was back in London and my mother and sister had only a bus ride on visiting day instead of a whole day's excursion.

There was a little incident at the Scrubs which, without wanting to harp on about it, goes back to the thorny issue of police corruption. I was working in the laundry with Freddie Foreman who was serving ten years for disposing of the body of Jack 'The Hat' McVitie, one of the Krays' victims. One morning Fred was called out for a visit, which was an unusual occurrence since visits are normally in the afternoons. Instead of taking him to the visiting room they took him to room 17, the office of the security screws. On entering he was confronted by two detectives.

'I don't have to talk to you cunts,' was as much as the detectives got by way of an interview and with that Fred turned on his heel and walked out.

The purpose of the visit had been to interview Fred over the murder of Ginger Marks and the police version of Fred's statement was 'I knew I should have murdered that bastard as well', naming a witness to the Marks murder. This was quite damaging verbal evidence if left unchallenged.

Shortly afterwards Fred was moved to Wandsworth and sent me a message telling me of his predicament. Because he was on the 'A' list Fred was accompanied by two screws on the visit and they had kept a log of his movements. I went to speak to an Assistant Governor, Bernie Fowler, I had quite a good relationship with and who was a pretty fair man. He checked the logs and found out the names of the two officers who had been present. Contrary to what you might expect, policemen and prison officers are not really kindred spirits and these two were prepared to make a statement saying Fred's version of the chat was the true account of what had transpired. The murder charge against Fred was not pursued.

The prison system is really quite a small world. The entire prison population of the UK back then, men, women and children, wouldn't have half-filled Wembley Stadium so it's not surprising you bump into people with whom you're acquainted. Debonair Ted was one such. During one of our recce missions on the bit of work with the train to Swindon we had been forced to abort due at an awful lot of police activity. It turned out that the body of a young girl had been discovered in a phone box not far from where I was parked up. Ted was responsible for the murder and was serving life when I spotted him, though I never had anything to do with him.

Train robbers had a certain amount of celebrity status and it wasn't unusual for weaker prisoners to try and pal you up in the hope of gaining a little reflected prestige. One afternoon in the canteen queue a bloke said to me 'I know you, don't I?'

'Don't think so mate,' I said

'Yeah, you go to St George's Gym, don't you,' he persisted.

'No, mate. What's your name?' I asked.

When he told me it rang a bell but I said no more and left it at that. Returning to my cell I went through a few back issues of the *Wandsworth Borough News*. Sure enough, there he was. Sexual assault on an elderly woman. Saucy bastard, trying to pal me up. I waited for my opportunity and a few days later gave him a sharp right hook to the jaw. Not long after his release he was re-arrested on a murder charge and got life.

Sundays in the unit were quite relaxed days. We were allowed 'free association' which meant we could wander around and have little group meetings in each other's cells without getting any hassle from the screws. One Sunday, 24th February, we had arranged a party. We'd managed to get hold of a large bottle of vodka, I'd acquired a bucket of fairly decent home-brewed hooch, Charlie and Jim Hussey had provided the peanuts, olives and a few bags of crisps. We were just coming under starter's orders when a screw appeared and told me to report to the governor's office.

The governor informed me that I had been given a compassionate visit, which never bodes well. It was unheard of to get a visit on a Sunday so something serious had happened and I went off to the visiting room full of trepidation.

My visitor was a great old pal, Ronnie Cisco, and he was heartbroken. His youngest daughter, Belinda, had been killed in an accident in the Canaries and he needed some help to get the body home. I gave him a phone number and the problem was solved. How I wished there was more I could have done for him. After all Ronnie had been the person who had acquired the oxy-arc torch we had needed in Cork and they were damned difficult to get hold of.

Needless to say I wasn't in much of a party mood by the time I got back to the cell. The lads were all pissed but they had been good enough to save me a decent cup of vodka which I really felt I needed. No sooner had I got it down my throat than my nemesis, Assistant Governor Howard Jones, a Welshman and a total prick, appeared in the cell doorway. Possibly he'd been alerted by Freddie Foreman's singing. He didn't say a word, just stood there, speechless, glaring at us.

'Sit down and have a drink or fuck off out, Jonesy,' said Jimmy Hussey.

I'd never got on with Jones since the day I arrived at The Scrubs four years earlier. He was one of those self-important petty officials who reserved his best endeavours for the likes of rapists and child molesters. After my back operation I was returned to work in the laundry where the humid atmosphere aggravated the problem. I spent months applying for a change of labour but Jones blocked me at every turn. In the end I even petitioned the Home Office but obviously Jones had a lot more clout than me and obliging career criminals wasn't on his list of priorities.

To say he was shocked would be an understatement. He turned on his heel and stormed out while we sat waiting for the heavy mob to arrive. Ten minutes later a senior officer, an experienced bloke and not a bad man, appeared. All he said was 'Time gentlemen please.' He defused what could have been quite a volatile situation realising the booze was all gone so evidence was a bit on the thin side. We heard no more about it.

It was often the way that the more experienced screws were prepared to take the line of least resistance. There was one old boy, Tom, who'd come into the prison service at a relatively late age. He'd worked as a gamekeeper somewhere up in Yorkshire and been made redundant. With the redundancy he'd not only lost his job but also his home so he signed up as a screw because it solved both problems and was a job with the minimum of academic requirements.

One day a pal invited me round to his cell to share a bottle of vodka. With the best part of the bottle finished Tom appeared in the doorway and he probably detected from our demeanour that we were a little the worse for wear. He walked around to my side of the table and tried to peer into my cup and my pal took the opportunity to demolish the remains of his cupful. Tom dashed around the table in an attempt to prevent him. The distraction allowed me the chance to demolish the remains of mine. Tom flew back and grabbed my cup to smell it and my pal snatched up the water jug containing the last dregs of the contraband and necked it. A fairly frustrated Tom stormed out of the cell taking my cup with him. I gave him a bit of a start and headed back to my own cell.

Ten minutes later Tom arrived, cup in hand.

'Is this your cup?' he asked.

'Well…' I said, 'it looks like a cup I used to have.' Thinking he might have some sort of forensic examination in mind I didn't really want to commit myself.

He walked over to my wash basin, picked up the water jug and swilled the cup out. Placing the cup on my washstand he walked out muttering something to the effect that he'd better not catch me again. Who wants to come to work every morning feeling that they're sat on a powder-keg, expecting any minute to get the contents of a piss-pot thrown over them – or worse. When you're dealing with people with not much to lose it's better to turn a blind eye when circumstances allow and the sensible screws usually did. Jonesy could have caused a riot in an empty house.

ON 11 MARCH 1975, my forty-fifth birthday, I received a card from Roy James with his very distinctive handwriting telling me that he had been given a date for parole, which was great news for all of us as we could now be optimistic about our own dates.

The same day I received much more upsetting news. Whilst moving a heater from one room to another my mother had had a stroke and when she collapsed she had broken her shoulder, her arm and her neck. She was also badly burnt and on the danger list in hospital. The governor granted me permission to visit her but my departure didn't go off without incident. In reception the Principal Officer produced a pair of handcuffs. I told him no fucking way was I going to visit my mother in handcuffs. For God's sake, I was eleven years into my sentence and expecting parole any minute, I was hardly going to have it away at that stage of the game. A phone call to the governor resolved the situation.

The police escort were remarkably cordial and at the hospital they discreetly disappeared and left me alone to see my mother, who looked terrible. I went and found a doctor and asked to be given it straight. He said that everything that was broken could be fixed but she would have to remain totally immobile for three months. I went and told her the prognosis and showed her the card from Roy, knowing she'd recognise his handwriting.

'I'll probably be home before you,' I told her.

'Bet you won't,' she said.

'How much do you bet?' I asked her.

'A hundred quid,' she replied.

It was a pleasure to pay her, eight months later.

My first two parole applications, in '73 and '74, had been refused but it was third time lucky and in 1975 it was granted. To be fair to Edmund Davies, being as high up as he was in the judiciary, he must have been well aware when he sentenced us that the parole system was only around the corner. Had he sentenced us to the par for the course of fifteen or eighteen years and with parole we were all back on the streets after five or six years, he and the whole establishment would have looked pretty stupid. No doubt the appeal court judges were in much the same position and had they reduced the sentences they would have finished up looking equally stupid.

11

The Aftermath

JOHN DALY, the one with the get-out-of-jail-free card, never got to enjoy his share of the spoils. The two people who were minding the money, presumably under the impression that he was going to be away for a very long time, made their own of it. Despite vigorous efforts to recover it he was unable to do so. One of the men died, apparently from natural causes and the other disappeared off the face of the earth. John turned his back on crime after his narrow escape at the trial and moved to Cornwall where he worked for forty years for a local council as a dustman and street cleaner. He died on 10 April 2013 from multiple organ failure after a long illness.

First to be released, in 1965, was John Wheater, the solicitor and Brian Field's boss, having served two years of his three-year sentence. He retired and went to live in Surrey.

He was followed by Brian and Lennie Field in 1967. They had each served three years and four months of their five-year sentences. Most people think that Brian played a fairly minor role in the robbery, bearing in mind his comparatively short sentence. Nothing could be further from the truth. Without Brian's information the whole scheme would never have gotten off the ground so he was a crucial part of the conspiracy.

On release he changed his name to Brian Carlton and disappeared for a while. Rumour had it that, in an effort to extort all or part of his share of the spoils, he was kidnapped and tortured by an ex-con who was released a few weeks before him. Bit pointless really since the police had recovered the bulk of his share before his arrest and what was left went on legal fees. The man thought to be behind the kidnap was later murdered. In 1979, at the age of forty-four, Brian and his third wife, Sian, were killed in a car crash. Returning from Wales on the M4 motorway, his Porsche was in collision with a Mercedes driven by the daughter of celebrity hairdresser Mr Teasy-Weasy (Raymond Bessone). The daughter, her husband and their two children were also killed. Because of his name change it was a few weeks before Brian's true identity was known.

The next to leave prison was the innocent Billy Boal but his misfortunes continued in as much as he left in a wooden box. Bill never gave up trying to prove his innocence and petitioned everyone petitionable: the Home Secretary, the Commission on Human Rights, the Council of Europe. At time of writing his family are preparing a file for the Criminal Case Review Committee in the hope of getting a posthumous pardon. When Bruce died earlier this year he left a note for Bill's family confirming that Bill took no part in the work or the conspiracy. Having served seven years of his fourteen year sentence, he died in 1970.

Roger Cordrey was the first of the robbery team to be freed. His conviction for robbery having been overturned he served eight years of his fourteen year sentence for handling and was released in 1971. I hadn't known Roger well before the robbery and had little contact with him after our releases but to the best of my knowledge he had no further run-ins with the Old Bill. He went back into the florist business having moved to the West Country.

BUSTER WAS RELEASED in 1975. The money from the train was spent before his arrest and he needed a job to fulfil his parole commitments so he opened a flower stall near Waterloo Station. British Leyland came up with an advertising campaign for the Mini which went 'nips in and out like Ronnie Biggs' and erected a huge hoarding right in front of Buster's stall. He had a minor run-in with the Old Bill when he was arrested for shoplifting from Harrods. Bit ironic really since at one time Buster had a contract with Harrods to supply the wigs worn by the shop-window mannequins. He was jailed for nine months and whilst in prison met up with a bloke who claimed to be a computer fraud expert. Computer fraud was still in its infancy back then and obviously Buster knew nothing about it but he got involved with this bloke on his release. It turned out the bloke was nothing but a conman and Buster lost the money he was talked into investing.

In 1987 a much romanticised version of his life story was made into a film, *Buster*, with Phil Collins playing his part. It portrayed Buster as a cross between a bumbling fool and a likeable rascal. Nothing could be further from the truth. Buster was a total professional and one of the staunchest people I ever worked with. Buster was far from impressed with the script and threatened to sue to stop production and was told to go ahead – the publicity would suit the producer fine. Bit like the time I sued the *People* and won and was awarded two pounds damages. The *People* had published an article alleging I had taken part in the London Airport robbery and since I'd been acquitted of that job it was libel. They also accused me of 'coercing an innocent and decent young woman' (Karin Field) into taking part in the Great Train Robbery. I won on both counts, hence the two quid damages. In the end Buster agreed to accept ten grand to make the script an 'authorised version' but it still bore little resemblance to the truth. Bruce was employed as an adviser on the film and was as little impressed by the final result as Buster had been.

Buster killed himself in 1995, hanging himself in a lock-up garage at Waterloo. I always had the feeling that Buster somehow felt embarrassed that he had received only fifteen years when Charlie and I got thirties but he really shouldn't have. In truth we were delighted for him. At the time of his death there was some talk that he was very concerned about an ongoing fraud investigation. Charlie had been involved in a big VAT scam so it's quite possible that that was what Buster was worried about.

They broke the mould when they made Buster and I miss him terribly.

Roy James came home in August, 1975 having served twelve years. He tried to get back into Formula 1 racing but had several crashes and was forced to give up the game. He went back to his trade as a silversmith and, through his friendship with Bernie Ecclestone, worked on a few Formula 1 trophies. Roy had written to Ecclestone before leaving prison asking for his help in getting back into the racing game but age had caught up with him and in any case he didn't have the finance. It was this connection that gave rise to the rumours that Ecclestone was the real financier of the robbery. When challenged about this, Ecclestone said, 'The Great Train Robbery? Wasn't enough money in it for me!'

Roy was arrested in 1981 with Charlie Wilson over a VAT fraud but wasn't charged. In 1993 he was arrested for shooting and wounding his ex-father-in-law and beating up his ex-wife. He was jailed for six years. Whilst in prison he underwent a triple heart bypass and was released in 1997, only to die within weeks, aged 62.

Jimmy Hussey and Tommy Wisbey were freed in early 1976. Tommy was arrested in '79 for playing a small role in a travellers' cheque fraud but was not returned to prison. In 1989 he was arrested over a cocaine smuggling operation after a kilo of coke was discovered in his house. Jimmy had been photographed earlier handing a parcel to him and was also arrested. Tommy was jailed for ten years and Jimmy for seven. Jimmy died from cancer on 13 November 2012, after a lengthy stay in a hospice. Tommy is still alive at time of writing.

Jimmy White's release also came in 1976, having served ten years of his eighteen year sentence. He had no further convictions and lived a quiet life until his death in 2012.

Bobby Welch was released in June 1976, the last, apart from Charlie, of those sentenced at Aylesbury to come home. During his sentence he was given a cartilage operation which was less than successful and he was destined to spend the rest of his life walking with a stick. He went back into the night club business and had no further run-ins with the Old Bill.

Bruce Reynolds was freed on parole in 1979 having served eleven years of his twenty-five year sentence. He had been divorced from his wife Frances whilst in prison and had a hard time adjusting when he came home. I spent a lot of time with him and introduced him to a girl with whom he had a relationship for a while. Eventually he was re-united with his wife but was re-arrested and convicted of playing a minor role in a drugs deal. He was sentenced to three years but this would prove to be his last conviction. He died peacefully in his sleep on 28 February 2013.

Charlie Wilson, having received one of the longest sentences and having been on the run for four years, was the last to be released. He came home just in time to get involved in the Great VAT Swindle or, as it was better known, simply 'The Gold'. This was a VAT fraud based on the buying and selling of gold and the pocketing of the VAT. Massive money was earned by a lot of people.

He moved to Spain, buying a run-down villa in San Pedro, outside Marbella, which he refurbished to a spectacular standard. On one of his trips home he was arrested over the VAT fraud and put on remand in Brixton. Penalties for VAT fraud weren't very severe because when the laws were drafted no-one envisioned anyone stealing vast amounts of money, but Charlie had a problem. If he was convicted he would be in violation of his parole and would have to return to prison to finish his thirty year sentence. In the end he agreed to forfeit the one hundred and sixty grand that HM Customs and Excise had confiscated from him in return for the charges being dropped. He was released having parted with ten grand more than his share from the train.

On 25 April 1990, the news hit the papers that Charlie had been shot dead at his villa the previous evening. There had been a fall-out and, although Charlie had only been on the periphery of the cannabis trade, this was the basis of the fall-out. A man had been arrested after a consignment of puff had been discovered in London. He asked Charlie if it would be in order for him to use as a defence that the puff had nothing to do with him but that it in fact belonged to a South Londoner who was at the time living in Amsterdam and had no intention of ever returning to the UK. Charlie said that he couldn't see what harm it would do. Apparently the South Londoner took a different view when he heard about it and hired a hitman called Danny Roff to have a word with Charlie. I was reliably informed that the murder was not intentional but was in fact 'a strong pull that went wrong'. Be that as it may, the fact remains that Charlie was dead. The South Londoner was later shot dead himself in the Midnight Lounge of the American Hotel in Amsterdam, and Roff copped it too some years later.

I wasn't able to go over to Streatham Cemetery for Charlie's funeral but Bruce, Roy James, Jimmy White, Buster and Bobby Welch all attended. Pat asked me to take care of the remaining two dogs as she felt she would never return to Spain and to the best of my knowledge she never has. The whole thing was a tragedy and Charlie is another that is sadly missed.

Terry Hogan gave up crime completely and went into the demolition business at which he became quite successful. He did his best to help Bruce when he came home from prison, finding a job for him in his business but Bruce wasn't the type to be happy to settle for a straight living. In the early nineties Terry began to suffer from depression, almost certainly brought on by the murder of Charlie Wilson and the suicide of Buster Edwards. In 1995 he too committed suicide, jumping from the window of his flat in London. He had only visited me in Mojacar a week or two earlier.

Unfortunately one mystery I can't resolve to anyone's satis-faction is who bashed Jack Mills but I can tell you who didn't. It certainly wasn't me. When the Piers Paul Read book *The Train Robbers* was ready to come out in 1978, W.H. Allen refused to publish it unless someone took responsibility for Mills's injuries. Buster, being Buster, stepped up and said it was him. It wasn't. On his deathbed Jimmy Hussey confessed to it but it wasn't him either. It was beginning to get a bit like 'I'm Spartacus' the way everyone wanted to take responsibility. Bruce was half a mile away with John Daly at the dwarf signal. Jimmy White and Roy James were making their way back to the bridge from where they had uncoupled the train. Roger Cordrey was twenty feet up a gantry tampering with the signal. Charlie was waiting at the bridge preparing to smash his way into the HVP as were Tommy Wisbey and Bobby Welch.

The exact location of everyone else is difficult to remember and don't forget there were a number of big men dressed similarly and wearing masks. It may sound very convenient but my opinion, which for once in my life coincides with the police opinion at the time, was that the man who actually struck the blow was one of the three robbers never arrested or identified. The money found in the Great Dover Street phone box was left by one of these three men and it is almost certain that he was the man responsible for Mills's injuries.

Tommy Butler refused to accept retirement at fifty-five and was determined to stay on until Bruce was caught, which put Frank Williams's nose out of joint as he was waiting to be promoted. He finally retired in 1968 and died on 20 April 1970, at the age of fifty-eight.

IN 2001 WE were all back in the newspapers when Ronnie Biggs decided to give himself up. By this time he was penniless, in very poor health and Bruce went over to Rio to accompany him home, together with Biggsy's son, Michael. The expenses and presumably a few quid, were paid by one of the red tops.

Whilst rehashing the story of the train the papers made mention that Jack Mills's death seven years after the robbery was a result of the injury he sustained during the robbery. This led to a letter, written by a certain S.R. Harvey of Manchester, being published in the *Times*. Quite who S.R. Harvey is and what his or her position is in the scheme of things I'm at a loss to know but it sounds so authoritative and is so relevant I feel it warrants reproducing in it entirety.

Unfair To Biggs

Coverage of Ronnie Biggs's return repeated the claims that train driver Jack Mills's death in 1970 was linked to the head injury he sustained during The Great Train Robbery. When Jack Mills died in Crewe from chronic lymphatic leukaemia complicated by bronchial pneumonia, the West Cheshire coroner announced, 'I am aware that Mr Mills sustained a head injury in the course of the train robbery in 1963. There is nothing to connect this injury to the cause of death.' On February 21th 1970, The Times published a letter from Peta Fordham, the wife of the barrister who defended Gordon Goody and Ronnie Biggs and author of a book on the train. She said that Jack Mills admitted to her that the worst injury he sustained was not from the coshing but from hitting his head on the wall of the train when he fell. When Mrs Fordham asked him why he had not said so in court and why he would not repeat what he had told a reporter – that the robbers had treated him 'like a gentleman' – Mr Mills replied 'Please don't repeat this as I've been warned that my pension would be affected if it ever got out.'

I think all that goes a long way to confirming all I said earlier about Jack Mills's injury and why the general public were led to believe it was much more serious than it was.

Peta Fordham had written the first, and arguably the worst, of the multitude of books about the robbery. To be fair to her she was restricted in what she could write by the fact that Bruce, Buster and Jimmy White were still on the run and it would be highly improper for a barrister's wife to mention anything about people who might yet have to face trial.

She sent me a copy of the book which was inscribed on the flyleaf, 'Don't look on this as the assassin's dagger but rather the surgeon's scalpel.' Although she was quite flattering to me in it I found it pretty hard going and not terribly accurate.

Ronnie would finally be granted parole on compassionate grounds in 2009 and died in 2013. I never felt any sympathy for Ron, and his exploits whilst on the run did none of us any favours with the authorities. The thing that really went against the grain as far as I'm concerned was when he stated in his book that I was the person who assaulted Mills. Aside from the fact it wasn't me, Biggs was in no position to know who the person responsible was. The timing of the book's publication, by accident or design, coincided with my parole hearing, which could have caused me untold damage. So, in a nutshell, fuck him.

I WAS RELEASED on 23 December 1975. Having served twelve Christmases inside it was nice to escape spending the thirteenth, if only by the skin of my teeth. However, even my release didn't go off without incident. On the Saturday morning an Assistant Governor Jones came into my cell to inform me that my parole had been granted. Normally parole results were given on a Friday lunchtime but the prison was in lockdown due to some sort of protest by the IRA prisoners, several of whom were on the roof hurling slates at the screws. Say what you want about the IRA but anyone who throws slates at screws can't be all bad.

These days prisoners are allowed all kinds of equipment – satellite TV, radios, CD players and the rest – but back then the only radio allowed was medium and long wave and that only after serving four years of a sentence. UHF and VHF were prohibited because they could pick up the communication radios of the staff. I had a set that could receive UHF concealed under my pillow and as the AG was standing there both his personal radio and the one under my pillow started squawking with messages from the screws below trying to quell the riot.

'What was that?' Jonesy asked.

'Fucked if I know,' I said.

'Bearing in mind I'm here to tell you your parole has been granted it might not be a bad time to start being truthful with me,' was Jonesy's advice.

With that he put his hand under the pillow, copped for the radio and left to go next door and give Jimmy Hussey the glad tidings.

The next morning Jimmy and I went down to the office to apply for pre-parole leave which was granted. After two days of debauchery we returned, looking at about ten days before we were home for good. On the Saturday morning my cell door wasn't opened so I rang the bell to find out what was going on.

'Sorry Gordon. I can't let you out,' said the screw. 'Jonesy has nicked you for contraband.' The bleeding radio!

I was taken down to chokey to await adjudication. On the way one of the screws said, 'You know you've done your parole now Goody, don't you.'

The lads I'd been sharing a dining table with for years, who included Jimmy Hussey, Buster, Freddie Foreman, Frank O'Connell, Billy Gentry and Georgie Smith, took exception to this remark, feeling loss of eight years' parole was a bit strong over an illicit radio. They began to voice their opinion. Forcefully. By the Sunday afternoon the wing was on the brink of an outright mutiny and I got a visit from another AG, Bernie Fowler, who was quite a nice chap. Jones was off-duty and Fowler asked me to return to the wing and try to put the lid on things. Our dining table, number four, was normally looked upon as something of a stabilising influence on the rest of the wing. We were all doing long sentences and generally caused the staff the minimum inconvenience. I went back and things began to return to normal. If Billy Gentry had had his way there'd have been a full scale riot but I managed to cool him down and the protest came to an end.

On the Monday morning I was up in front of the governor who was about as accommodating as a prison governor ever gets. Not being inclined to go against his assistant he was unable to overlook the offence. Instead he sentenced me to fifteen days in the punishment block and told me that if it passed without incident no reference would be made to the parole board.

By coincidence on my last night in the Scrubs a concert had been arranged and the line-up included George Melly, Kathy Kirby, Larry Adler and David Frost. Not a bad going-away party. Kathy Kirby was about to make a comeback after recovering from an alcohol problem and she received a standing ovation. She was so moved she wound up crying.

As I walked out of the gatehouse the next morning Norman Honey, the No. 1 Governor, appeared to wish me good luck and tell me not to come back. He also gave me a slip of paper which turned out to be David Frost's phone number. At the time he was hosting *Late Night with Frost* on London Weekend and wanted me to appear on the show. Not really my thing and I never did get around to phoning him.

12

The Ulsterman

PADDY MCKENNA, THE Ulsterman, was probably the most fortunate of any of us. He got his full share of the proceeds and avoided the monumental legal expenses we all had.

I had strong reservations about naming Paddy at all and had to do a lot of soul-searching before doing so. It wasn't just my habitual refusal to name comrades that gave me concern. Just as worrying was, would I be believed? There was a previous episode with the Piers Paul Read book, where the story floated that an ex-Nazi called Otto Skorzeny masterminded the robbery was subsequently proved to be bollocks. Perhaps my new revelations would be looked on with scepticism bearing in mind the only people who ever met Paddy, at least in his role as the Ulsterman, were Brian Field, Buster and myself. Brian and Buster are long gone so in reality there is only God and myself who know if there is any truth in the Ulsterman story.

Then a funny thing happened. I was approached by a TV company and asked if I would be interested in taking part in a documentary to coincide with the fiftieth anniversary of the robbery. When the producers discovered I was in a position to name the Ulsterman they set about trying to verify his identity.

A private investigator, Martin Young, a member of the Association of British Investigators, was employed to see if he could track down any record of a Paddy McKenna working for the Post Office at the time of the robbery. It was a mammoth task and the trail led down a lot of blind alleys. Starting with just a name, and a fairly common one at that, an approximate age and an approximate place of birth the list of possibilities ran into the hundreds. Some could be eliminated quite easily as too young, too old or had died before the robbery took place. Even so, by Mr Young's own admission, it had got to the stage of little more than shots in the dark.

A researcher, Ariel Bruce, took up the hunt and there followed months of work trolling through birth, marriage and death certificates and correlating them with post office work records. Ms Bruce was concerned that my recollection of Paddy's age could have been well out. At the time of the robbery I was thirty-three and I estimated Paddy to be ten or fifteen years older than me. Ms Bruce decided to err on the side of caution and extended the age frame to twenty years meaning Paddy could have been as old as fifty-three and his date of birth as early as 1910. Of course this made the potential candidate pool proportionally bigger.

Immediately after the robbery, of the underworld tips given to the police a number mention both an Irishman and a postal worker being the source of the information. I found this amazing because for certain not one word had been mentioned to anyone by Brian, Buster or myself. Then I remembered the mysterious Mark who had turned up on the very first meet with Brian. The same Mark who had been paid to burn down the farm and had failed to do so.

Besides underworld tips, right from the start people as high as Reginald Bevin, the Postmaster General, admitted that they 'couldn't rule out' the possibility of it being an inside job. In a funny way the police having this information appeared to be an advantage to Ms Bruce. The transport police spent hundreds if not thousands of man hours keeping surveillance on dozens of postal workers connected to the train and members of their families. Ms Bruce went through half a shelf of these records available under the Freedom of Information Act at the National Archives. The detail was amazing. Names, addresses, dates of birth, car registration numbers, associates, accents, habits – did they drink, did they gamble, did they frequent prostitutes. Unfortunately the search was fruitless. Not one single Patrick McKenna was amongst the suspects. Some-how Paddy had stayed under the radar.

Eventually Ms Bruce travelled to Northern Ireland with a list of eight possible candidates, five of whom could be elimanated quite quickly for various reasons. The remaining three had birth dates of 1907, 1917 and 1929, all of which were within the outside parameters she had set.

On the eventual shortlist there was one man who stood out. There was a Patrick McKenna who was born on 27 September 1917. His birth certificate was bought which gave access to his parents' names and from there his siblings, his employment record and his war service. He had joined the post service in 1933 at the age of fourteen as a messenger. At the start of the Second World War he had joined the RAF and he re-joined the post office in London at the end of hostilities. He married a girl from Manchester at Islington Registry Office in 1949 at which time he lived at Southall Road, Beckenham – only ten minutes' walk from where we had the meeting at Finsbury Park.

By 1963, McKenna was employed at the main sorting office in Newton Street, Manchester, which was where he learned of the travelling post office and the HVP carriage. So, it would seem the information came from Manchester and not London as I had always assumed.

One day during the filming of the documentary at my house in Vera, live on camera, the director produced some photos and asked me if I recognised anyone. Looking at the face of the man I hadn't seen in fifty years was one of the few occasions in my life when I was completely lost for words. Nobody knows better than me that eye-witness identification is notoriously unreliable. Usually an eye-witness gets little more than a brief glance at a suspect during a fairly traumatic experience. But this was different, we are talking of a man I had met numerous times for lengthy periods of time even if it was fifty years in the past.

Eventually I said that I was ninety-nine per cent sure that I was holding a picture of the Ulsterman. I didn't want to say one hundred per cent because I don't know if Paddy has any family still living and if so I wanted to be able to give them a little wriggle-room. Now they can say, 'Well, even Gordon wasn't a hundred per cent sure it was Paddy.'

In 1974, at the age of fifty-seven, McKenna took early retirement due to ill-health at which time he was living in Salford, Greater Manchester. He spent the rest of his life living in very modest circumstances in a working-class neighbourhood in a back-to-back, Coronation Street-style house until his death in 1995. His death certificate records his occupation as 'retired postal executive', a position he rose to in the years after the train robbery. He died without leaving a will, which leaves another mystery – if he didn't spend it, what happened to his share, some £3 million at today's values? His surviving family maintain they saw no sign of unexplained wealth.

In the years prior to the robbery there was much resentment amongst postal workers at what they perceived to be a very cavalier attitude by management to the workers' safety. Millions of pounds were being shuffled around the country on a daily basis with the bare minimum of security. It may well be that Paddy's prime motivation wasn't the money itself but more a desire to stick two fingers up at the Railways Board.

I can only speculate but there is one other possibility. Paddy was a staunch Roman Catholic originating from Northern Ireland. Given the climate at the time maybe a donation was made to a political organisation or maybe a religious organisation. It's known that Paddy was involved with several charitable organisations and even when in failing health he attended church regularly. Maybe there is a small village church somewhere in Northern Ireland with a spectacular stained glass window, possibly depicting a locomotive.

13

Freedom

So THAT WAS that and, barring the weekly chore of visiting my parole officer, I was a free man and I went to live at my mother's house in Putney. I was in a better position financially than most of the crew, having three houses, the hairdressers, a second-hand furniture shop and some cash. I'd relax and enjoy Christmas before making any decisions as to what the future might hold.

A fair proportion of the train proceeds had been disipated whilst I was in prison. The trial expenses were crippling. I'd employed the best solicitors, barristers and QC that money could buy for the longest trial in British legal history. Then had to do it all over again for the appeal. Not that I begrudged it, if you can't spend money on your own defence what can you spend it on? The whole legal team worked as hard as anyone could but given the political nature of the charges they were up against it from the start.

On top of that there were the expenses of being in prison itself. The little luxuries I treated myself to, like the odd bottle of vodka, didn't come cheap. You can't expect a screw or civilian instructor to risk job and pension for nothing. Some of my visitors, particularly my mother, wouldn't be in a position to pay the costs of travelling to see me and needed some assistance. Don't forget I was away twelve years and it all adds up, but that's all part of the game.

It's hard to describe the sensation of freedom to anyone who has never experienced the loss of it. In some ways things had changed unrecognisably in the twelve years I'd been away and in others it was like time had stood still. I visited a lot of my old haunts and caught up with a lot of my old pals. Bruce, of course, was still away and looked like being so for some time to come. Charlie likewise, but Buster was home and we spent a good deal of time together.

A pub we used frequently was the Turk's Head, in Chelsea, owned by a pal of mine, Terry Mainment, who did some work in the film industry and knew loads of celebrities. I suppose it's fair to say myself and Buster had a minor celebrity status at this point. One day Buster phoned me to come for a drink with the model Twiggy and her husband. Most people remember Twiggy as the waif-like figure from the early sixties but when I met her she was an absolute stunner. By this time she had parted ways with her manager Justin de Villeneuve. Actually his real name was Nigel Davies but he thought Justin de Villeneuve sounded better and who could blame him. The American actor Stacy Keach was in the company as well. In 1984 he would be arrested at Heathrow carrying a few grams of cocaine in a shaving cream container. He got nine months and during his sentence one of those jailhouse snitches palled him up. After Keach's release the snitch sold his story to the *News of the World* claiming he had been supplying Keach with drugs during his prison sentence. Probably all bollocks and I dropped Stacy a line assuring him not all ex-cons were that despicable.

One afternoon I was driving through the West End when my attention was distracted by a particularly stunning young lady in a very short miniskirt. Next thing I knew I'd driven up the arse of the car in front. The driver jumped out in a pretty irate mood but when I extended my six-foot-four frame from my Jag he calmed down a bit. It was only then that I realised that the unfortunate chap was none other than Johnny Briggs who at the time played a leading part in *Coronation Street*. I haven't read his memoirs myself but I've been told that he recalled the incident therein and he goes on to say that we got chatting and I offered him a bit of work on a bank job I was planning. Aside from the fact that I was on sabbatical from the bank game, being the cautious chap I am the chances of me offering work to a total stranger are less than remote.

IN 1976 SIX of us – me, Buster, Jimmy White, Roy James, Bobby Welch, Tommy Wisbey – together with South African literary agent Gary Van Dyke had a meeting at the London offices of W.H. Allen & Co, book publishers. Bruce and Charlie were still in custody and Biggsy was still on the trot in Rio. We were there to discuss a project to write a book about the train robbery with Piers Paul Read. I had more than slight concerns about the whole idea. In the first place if it could have any detrimental effect on Bruce and Charlie's likelihood of parole it was a non-starter. I was also worried that we might be required to make admissions that could lead to further problems with the Old Bill or even the parole board. On the other hand, unlike myself, most of the lads were on the floor financially speaking so if a few quid could be earned I was obliged to give it at least consideration.

FROM THE PUBLISHERS' point of view the problem was that there had already been several books and a couple of films made about the robbery. Was there really anything new to say that would warrant the expense of rehashing it all again? To get around this a story was concocted that a 'Mr Big' had planned and financed the job to the tune of £100,000 in exchange for a £1 million of the proceeds.

The name chosen for this mythical 'Mr Big' was Otto Skorzeny, an Austrian who had risen to Colonel in the SS during the war. He was one of Hitler's favourites and had led the mission to rescue the deposed Italian dictator Mussolini. He was also one of the leaders of Odessa, the organisation that spirited wanted Nazis to safety in South America which meant he would have had access to the funds to finance the robbery. The fact that Buster and Biggsy had undergone plastic surgery in Germany performed by a doctor who had previously done work for Odessa gave a little bit of credence to the hoax.

Of course all this was utter bollocks. Bruce, Buster, Charlie and I did most of the planning and none of us was short of money. By this time Skorzeny was dead so he wasn't in a position to challenge any of our allegations. Unfortunately the ruse was exposed long before the book went to print but in any event it had reasonable sales and a crust was earned. Other than the mythical financier, the book was fairly accurate. Years later Bruce would write his own story, *The Autobiography Of A Thief*, which was also quite successful.

The robbery business was one of the things that had changed dramatically during the years I'd been away. Firearms had become much more commonplace and not just amongst the robbers: the new specialist Robbery Squad carried guns on a routine basis.

As I said, I wasn't stuck for money but, in common with a lot of the people I worked with, for me the robbery game was never just about the money. The excitement, the planning, the clandestine meets, the cryptic phone calls, the fabrication of alibis were all part of the intrigue. Although alibi fabrication is pretty much Rule 101 I must admit I didn't do a wonderful job of my alibi for the train but that was just one of those times when circumstances conspired to send things awry. It sometimes turned out that way even when quite elaborate lengths were gone to.

I had a pal who went on a bit of work at a bank in the West End. The day before the robbery he arranged for a telegram to be sent from Scotland informing him that a relative was seriously ill. He then hopped a flight to Glasgow, carefully safeguarding his boarding pass. That night he got a pal to drive him back to London to be on the plot for the work the following night. The job was successful and a considerable sum was liberated but the pal had spent so long driving about waiting for him he was no sooner in the car than they ran out of petrol. By now it was six in the morning and he was walking through his own manor trying to thumb a lift to a petrol station. Had anyone spotted him all his careful planning would have been in the toilet.

Fortunately no-one did but the tale didn't have a happy ending. One of his co-workers was Bertie Smalls who would later become Britain's first supergrasses. When he went over he put all his pals in the mire, alibi or no alibi.

One pleasant innovation was Sir Robert Mark's appointment to the role of Metropolitan Police Commissioner. I'd had a soft spot for Sir Robert since the day he made a speech in Canada at the annual Chief Constables' Conference when he said, 'There are many worse people on the streets of London than the train robbers.' I had this speech reproduced and all of us included it in our next parole application. I'm convinced it carried a lot of weight with the parole board.

When Sir Robert was appointed in 1972 his first priority was to root out the widespread corruption in the London police, particularly at West End Central, the station in Mayfair that policed the Soho area.

Allegations of fit-ups at West End Central were rife and despite numerous inquiries few charges were ever brought. One notable exception was the case of Detective Sergeant Harold 'Tanky' Challenor who was a bona-fide war hero having been awarded the Military Medal whilst serving with the SAS behind enemy lines in Italy. He joined the Met in 1962 and had a phenomenal arrest and conviction rate, in one seven month period notching up one hundred successes. How he maintained this rate was quite simply by beating confessions out of suspects and when that didn't work, planting evidence. He was once accused of beating a black suspect to the rhythm of 'Bongo, bongo, bongo. I don't want to leave the Congo' but no charges were brought.

Tanky came a cropper when he was on duty at a demonstration outside Claridge's. He arrested Donald Rooum, a cartoonist from the *Peace News*, telling him, 'You're nicked my beauty,' and punching him in the head. Tanky then planted a half brick in Rooum's possessions, saying, 'My, my. Carrying an offensive weapon. That'll get you a two stretch.'

Unfortunately for Tanky, Rooum knew a little about forensics and instructed his solicitor to have the pockets of his clothes examined for brick dust and damage. Since there was none Rooum was acquitted and Tanky was charged with corruption. However, by the time of his trial at the Old Bailey he was diagnosed as suffering from a combination of paranoid schizophrenia and post-traumatic stress disorder and was declared unfit to plead. He was sacked and spent a few months in a psychiatric ward but his three co-accused officers were each jailed for three years.

With the arrival of Sir Robert Mark these practices became much less frequent. Even so, all this was something of a double-edged sword. Whilst your chances of being fitted-up were diminished it was equally true that your chances of bunging a few quid to an obliging cozzer for a bit of evidence tampering were also reduced.

So, all in all, maybe at the age of forty-five I'd have to consider a career change. Maybe a leopard can't change his spots but he can change his hunting ground if the need arises.

14

Spain

DURING MY TIME in prison I had spent quite a bit of time studying Spanish since it had always been an ambition to spend some time in a Latin country. If not Spain possibly South America. During my sentence I had got friendly with a Spanish lad, Juan, who never stopped telling me of the idyllic lifestyle of his home region of Andalucía so I travelled over to Mojacar in Almeria on Spain's eastern Costa del Sol. The Costa Del Crime legend was still a few years away but already a lot of expats were taking up residency, many of them from my old stamping grounds in the West End.

I had no great hankering for the fleshpots of Marbella and the western Costas. It's a sad fact of life that where successful villains congregate you're very likely to find grasses and, besides anything else, I was in a different position to a lot of Marbella residents in as much as I had no outstanding complications with the Old Bill. Almeria was twenty or thirty years behind Malaga and the rural lifestyle suited me perfectly. There were few cars and not much in the way of roads. Local deliveries were made by donkey and cart. To make a phone call you had to travel into the village and queue up to be connected through a switchboard. I found all this an asset rather than a disadvantage. One thing I did miss was English television and it would be ten years before Sky came into being. Eventually a German called Hans set himself up in the satellite television business and naturally enough he was soon referred to by everyone as 'Hans That Does Dishes'.

I rented an apartment on the seafront in Mojacar which at the time was a sleepy fishing village. For this place I paid the princely sum of forty quid a month. After a few years I bought the place paying nine grand and was destined to live there for the next twenty years. A few years after I bought it my brother bought one in the same block paying thirty-five grand so I must have done something right.

It's hard to describe how I spent my days. Doing very little pretty much sums it up. I'd go to bed late which meant I surfaced late and a leisurely breakfast at lunchtime was how things usually worked out. The beach, beach bars and al fresco dining passed the afternoon and early evening with any of the numerous expat bars being the later venues.

I'd always been keen on fly fishing and whilst in prison making flies had been a hobby that took up a lot of my time. I'd become quite proficient at it. There wasn't much opportunity for fly fishing on the coast so I gave sea fishing a go, renting a small boat, but I never really took to it. One pastime I did enjoy was taking country walks and I spent a lot of time in this pursuit. Once out of the village the birds and wildlife were abundant, the air was clean and you could walk for miles without seeing a soul. Far cry from central London.

The cost of living in Spain was low but, although I was quite comfortable for money, I was getting a bit concerned that there was nothing coming in. In common with a lot of expats with no trade to speak of I invested in a bar. It didn't earn any fortunes but when you're spending time working you're not spending money. Also, you're getting your booze wholesale.

It very soon became apparent that the one opportunity in Spain for an illicit earn was the cannabis trade, or the puff job as its practitioners referred to it. There were miles and miles of deserted beaches all along the coast of Almeria province and for years smugglers had been bringing gear over from Morocco and landing it at night. It was all very hit and miss back in the seventies, both on the part of the smugglers and of the forces of law and order. The customs service – La Aduana – was very under-manned, very poorly equipped and very badly paid. The smugglers were, by and large, inexperienced chancers and cowboys just giving it a go. In any case the penalties if you got caught weren't very severe and Spain was still quite corrupt back then. Anyone who got nicked, provided he had some money, wouldn't be spending much time in prison.

My first real introduction to the puff job came through an acquaintance called Freddie Jackson who was living in Almeria because it was so antiquated he thought the chances of taking a tumble there were much more limited than Malaga and Cadiz. Swings and roundabouts really. The Med tapers to a point, being at its narrowest at the Straits of Gibraltar where it's only nine miles wide. A straight line from Nador on the Moroccan coast to Almeria is more like two hundred miles and halfway across is a small island called Alboran which is some sort of a Spanish naval base. This means a half-hour dash on a high-speed launch becomes a twenty-four-hour expedition on a sail-boat. However, provided you give Alboran a wide berth you'd be unlucky to encounter any sort of reception committee on arrival. Hence Freddie's appearance on the scene.

One evening over a drink Freddie asked me if I was interested in a bit of work. He said he had some gear coming over and if I'd unload it and get it off the beach he was prepared to pay me fifty quid a kilo. There would be 560 key so we were talking £28,000 wages. I said I'd be delighted, realising that this was vastly more wages than the going rate for the job. There was a young chap I had a drink with now and again who wasn't doing much and was usually stuck for dough. I subcontracted the work to him at £20 a key which was more like the going rate. My only involvement was keeping an eye on the operation from a half mile distance. The job went off without a hitch – well, one small hitch. One of his duties was to sink the dinghy, which he stabbed but he neglected to open the petrol cap and next morning it had floated up on the beach. Didn't seem to cause much concern to anyone.

Let's just make a little comparison. If four or five of us went out to rob a bank, to net £28,000 apiece the first thing we'd have to do is find somewhere we could steal a hundred and fifty grand or so. A daunting enough task in itself. Take into account we'd be risking fifteen or eighteen years in the nick and, not insignificantly, a very real chance of getting shot. On the other hand, had the bit of beach work gone boss-eyed we'd probably be looking at a month or two on remand waiting for bail and then another few quid to make the paperwork disappear. Bit of a no-brainer really, isn't it. Over the next few months I oversaw two more bits of work for Freddie but like most good things in life the work didn't last forever and at the end of the season we drifted apart.

Knowing the people I know back home it's not really surprising that I'd had a few enquiries as to whether I'd be in a position to put my hands on a bit of puff. Now that I did know of availability I was reluctant to get into the re-sale end of things. The thing that worried me was the total disregard people, even normally sensible people, gave to security when it came to a bit of puff. Look around any prison exercise yard anywhere in the world and the vast majority of people are there because they couldn't keep their business to themselves.

Anyway, the big money seemed to come from exporting the gear back to England. It didn't take a cast of thousands, all it needed was a supplier, someone with a form of transport and someone who could confidently handle the sales back home. A tight little firm that nobody outside needed to know anything about. And we weren't talking vast amounts of gear. In quantity puff in Almeria was making about £700 a kilo and the wholesale price in London was in excess of £2,000 a kilo. Even allowing for the traditional £200 a kilo transport fee you would be more or less tripling your money. If, over a period, I could get twenty-five kilos home three times we're talking as much money as I received as my corner of the train robbery. All I had to do was recruit a supplier, a salesman and find some form of transport.

One morning I was on the balcony of my apartment having my early morning cup of tea and I spotted two removal lorries parked across the road. They were parked back to back and were so close together the company logos seemed to run into each other making the whole thing appear to be one enormous vehicle. It was such an amusing sight I took a photo. That afternoon in a bar I got into conversation with the drivers and gave them a copy of the photo which the company later adopted for their letterheads.

The lorries came over every couple weeks and I got quite pally with the drivers and before long I was able to pick their brains about how the company functioned. People would phone the company and book space on the vehicles to send any sort of consignment back to the UK The consignments could be dropped off directly to the drivers and often were made up of furniture and bulky personal effects of expats returning to the UK Hmmm. As discreetly as possible I pumped them about what the procedure was like when they arrived at British customs and was delighted to hear that they rarely got a look at. Apparently, in their early days they had had a spin or two but since nothing untoward had been discovered and since they passed through the same port on a regular basis they generally went through with little more than a nod.

Through a pal of mine I was introduced to a bloke called Billy Mae, an ex-pro middleweight boxer, who was in the puff game. Although Billy lived in Torremolinos he did most of his graft around Almeria, feeling, quite rightly, that he was less likely to finish up being the talk of the wash-house here than in Malaga. We had a chat and not only could he supply the product, he had people ready to purchase it if and when it arrived home.

I went out and bought a vacuum packer and we packed sixty key into three tea-chests, camouflaging it with bedding, books and a few wrapped ornaments. We paid a young lad to deliver the boxes to the lorry and gave him the address supplied to us by the people in England. We sat back to wait and a fortnight later the good news arrived: after an investment of fourteen grand each for the three of us we had £120,000 to cut up with very little in the way of expenses. Didn't seem a bad game, this puff job.

We used the transport company several more times. Billy and I were quite happy keeping our business on a small scale. The logistics were very simple with no need for pallets, fork-lifts or warehouses as were needed by the large-scale operators. Also, if something did go amiss the loss wouldn't be a huge body blow and even if the mishap occurred in England no great amounts of bird would be given out.

Next we started experimenting with making stashes in cars and had a fair degree of success. All very old-hat and these days you wouldn't last two minutes with such naive transport but back then things were a lot less sophisticated. Door panels were our first option and we got a parcel home a couple of times. Then I got hold of a fairly inventive welder who was very adept at cutting and welding quite well concealed stashes into boots, undercarriages and wings.

Between buying the car, doing the work, wrapping and packing the gear, waiting for it to get home and waiting for the money to get back over we were managing a bit of work every six or eight weeks. Of course we did have a few calamities, such is the nature of the game, but all in all we did very well and I was delighted with my new profession.

One day I was driving a car to our lock-up to load the gear into the carefully prepared stash. I pulled up a bit abruptly at a set of traffic lights but unfortunately a tipper truck travelling behind wasn't quite so abrupt and smashed into the rear, demolishing the boot. Our carefully prepared stash was now plainly visible for the world to see. Next minute a Guardia Civil jeep pulled up but happily his only concern was to see if anyone was hurt and he didn't even give the damage a look at. There was hardly a scratch on the tipper truck and I told the driver not to bother with insurance, that I'd have it repaired myself, which seemed to suit him fine. I certainly wouldn't be wanting an insurance assessor coming around to inspect this particular vehicle. As it turned out the chassis was twisted and the car was a write-off so I had it chopped up and no-one was ever any the wiser. Could have been worse, it could have happened on the way back from the lock-up and there'd have been fifty key of puff scattered over the road.

Actually, that very thing happened to a pal of mine in Liverpool. A truck ran up his arse, the stash burst open and a hundred key was scattered all over Upper Parliament Street. Not only did it cost him two hundred grand, he was nicked and got a two stretch.

As I said, I wasn't a big fan of Marbella and its neighbourhood but that doesn't mean I never went there. I'd visit Charlie quite often which would lead to a drink in one of the less high-profile bars and after all Marbella was the capital of the European puff game. Just as well to keep one's finger on the pulse of things. Besides Charlie there were a good few people who had been involved in the 'Great VAT Swindle' which was basically the buying and selling of gold and the pocketing of the VAT. Millions had been earned and when the bubble burst a good many of those involved arrived on the coast with their ill-gotten gains. Apart from Charlie I don't know of anyone being nicked over it and he got away with surrendering a hundred and sixty grand and having the charges dropped. Freddie Foreman, who had been in The Scrubs with me, and his partner, Ronnie Knight, who were both suspected of the

£6 million Security Express robbery at Shoreditch, were also living there.

On one of my trips to Marbella several of us went for a meal in an Argentinian steak house. There's a good few of these places around Marbella and pretty much all of them serve great steaks at very reasonable prices. Amongst the group was a Spanish girl from Madrid that I saw on a semi-casual basis. This girl had a big affection for smoking opium and this night, after a fair consumption of alcohol, she talked me into experimenting with it. This was the weirdest experience of my life. I can remember being in the toilet, perfectly awake but totally unable to move and in some sort of a cold sweat. One of those out-of-body experiences. The sensation lasted about ten minutes before I calmed down sufficiently to return to the table. That was the first and last time I ever touched opium and I didn't see much of the girl afterwards either.

One time, in 1986, I was down there for a couple of days and bumped into an old pal from London. Not surprisingly he was in the business as well and he began to tell me a story about a parcel of puff he'd bought that was of a fairly indifferent quality. Quality in the puff job is one of the biggest nightmares. If a farmer in Morocco is committed to supplying a ton but the crop he's planted only yields eight hundred he'll do his utmost to stretch the last gram out of it which means the last couple of hundred will be very suspect. Each quarter kilo bar has an embossed stamp to identify it – maybe a leaf, or a star, car insignia were quite fashionable, Merc, Ferrari and so on. All this means that there could well be a ton of gear on the market eight hundred of which are perfectly acceptable but as soon as someone discovers a bar of the crap the whole parcel has a bad name. The word goes around like wildfire – have nothing to do with, say, 'Ferrari', it's crap.

This pal of mine was one of the unfortunates who had finished up with fifty key of the tail-end and had been struggling for weeks to try and make something of it. It had been in and out and back in again so many times it was reduced to about forty-four key by this stage with so many people taking samples. He had come to the conclusion it was time to bite the bullet and sling the remainder on the tip rather than keep pulling up expenses to have it looked after. He asked me if I would come and give him a lift to get it into the car and go and dump it. Didn't seem like a massive task and off we went.

We drove to an underground car-park beneath a block of flats in Marbella and went up in the lift to fetch the gear. Slinging the two holdalls in the boot we set off for the tip but when we got to the top of the ramp there was a squeal of brakes and a squad car accompanied by a plain-clothes car boxed us in. We were nicked and taken to Marbella police station. After the usual rigmarole of photographs and finger-prints we were thrown in a cell where I gave myself a severe kick up the arse for getting involved in the first place.

A few hours later the head honcho opened the door and called me into his office. He told me to take a seat and said he'd checked me out and was well aware of exactly who I was. This was no major piece of detective work because, never thinking I'd be up to any sort of mischief, I was using a passport in my own name. He went on to say that if I wanted I was free to go. Jolly decent of him and I thanked him profusely but he then said that I had to understand that from then on I was working for him. This goes a long way to confirming what I said about always finding grasses where successful villains congregate. If he made that offer to me how many other people had he made it to? I was returned to the cell and, after a brief court appearance a few days later, off we went to Malaga nick.

I spoke earlier of what dismal places the likes of Strangeways and Durham are but Malaga nick gives a whole new perspective on dismal. The place was built in the early 1800s and hasn't improved with age. In a British prison the very first thing on arrival is a bath, your clothes are put in a cardboard box and a prison uniform is issued. Anyone who looks a bit questionable is given a fume-bath in case of body lice. None of these tiresome formalities in a Spanish prison but a couple of Spaniards who arrived with us showed us the ropes. The first job was to run a lighter over the foam-rubber mattress which produced an interesting crackling noise as the bed bugs exploded. Toilet facilities were a hole in the corner with two embossed footprints to show you where to squat. Or maybe they'd simply worn there over the years. The food was appalling. When we arrived on the first day we saw what appeared to be the remnants of dinner and my pal remarked how unfortunate we were to have missed dinner. It turned out that it was dinner. Food, sanitation and bed bugs apart there's nothing terribly arduous about a Spanish prison. There's no obligation to work. In fact there's very little in the way of work even if you felt that way inclined and the day is spent ambling around the exercise yard, or patio as they refer to it. As long as you've got money you can buy pretty much anything you need but I certainly wouldn't want to be in a Spanish jail broke. God knows how you'd survive.

We weren't housed in cells but in dormitories, called brigadas, with twenty-eight bunks in tiers. The one thing in the way of luxury was a fairly dilapidated TV but this was to give rise to my first run-in with the local mafia. The first night I was lying on my bunk watching some mildly interesting documentary when a big fat slob got up and changed the channel. Being a newbie I didn't feel it was my place to make an issue of it but when it happened again the next night I thought it was time to draw a line in the sand. I got up and changed it back. I don't think Fatso was used to having his authority undermined and there was a bit of a shocked silence. I'm six foot four and I'd like to think in better condition than Fatso. On the other hand he did have a few pals. On the third hand – can you say 'on the third hand'? I don't know, anyway – besides my pal and me there were two other Brits, both fairly well built, and a couple of Dutchmen, who all seemed to think that a regime change wouldn't be out of order. Things got a little heated and at one point pistols at dawn seemed the likely outcome. However, after a bit of bawling and shouting it was agreed that in future before the channel was changed a vote would be taken. I don't recall an awful lot of votes actually being taken but that's not the point. If you don't make a stand now and again in prison you'll get walked all over. Strangely enough I got quite pally with Fatso and a bit of mutual respect grew up.

It probably doesn't come as much of a surprise to hear that prisons are full of thieves but in an English gaol stealing from your fellow prisoners is very much frowned upon and dire consequences can befall transgressors. Apparently Spaniards aren't so picky about etiquette and will nick anything they can lay their hands on. If you turn your back for a couple of seconds shirts, shoes, jackets and anything else of value – even soap, toothpaste and shampoo – will all disappear. This practice was considered particularly acceptable when the victims were foreigners.

Of course the person that has the most use for the stolen clothing is the person who owned it so in pretty short order an emissary might well arrive and suggest that for some small compensation he could possibly assist in its recovery. This serves a dual purpose. In the first place the villains have a small earn and in the second place it means the clothing will be available to be stolen again in next to no time.

By the third or fourth time of re-buying the same collection of clothes I decided it was time to take some action. I got together with the three or four other expats in the brigada and we arranged to form a sort of rota system whereby whenever we were going to the exercise yard or the showers or on a visit, one of us would remain on guard-duty.

This all worked out quite well and for a time very little went missing but as usual in times of tranquillity one tends to let one's guard down. As luck would have it, it was my turn on duty when disaster struck. While the rest of the lads went to the yard I remained on parade. It was a lovely summer's day but the heat must have caused me to get drowsy and before I knew it I'd dozed off. I was awoken by the lads' return only to find that the bulk of our collective possessions had disappeared.

This left me in a very embarrassing position, feeling quite rightly that I had let the lads down and was obliged to make a stand. Fuck the consequences. I've often found that when severely outnumbered in a confrontation the best policy is to challenge the biggest and ugliest of your opponents. In this case it turned out to be the TV channel-hopper I'd had the previous run-in with.

Knives – or 'shivs' – are fairly endemic in Spanish nicks and a tear-up of a serious nature seemed very much on the cards. For a change the fickle finger of fate took a turn in my direction when the brigada door flew open and in marched a screw.

'Goody! Libertad!' he shouted.

My bail had come through and at this point I couldn't have cared less about my missing gear. I told them they could keep whatever they'd nicked and I'd throw in my radio and anything else they hadn't already nicked in return for the gear belonging to the rest of the lads. This was deemed an amicable resolution and we parted on good terms. Don't know how long it was before normal service was resumed but my days of guard duty were over.

SPANISH POLICE DON'T have a big reputation for fitting people up. The rule seemed to be that if they fell over you, you were nicked, and if someone said you'd done something, you had to prove you hadn't. Bribery however was rife and it was far from unusual for brown paper packages to change hands between police, briefs, prosecutors and even judges. That changed a lot when Spain joined the EU in 1986. That same year Colonel Luis Roldán, the head of the Guardia Civil, absconded to Mexico with around twenty million euros. It took the Spanish government ten years to get him back and he wound up with a sentence of thirty-one years. He was released after serving less than fifteen and hardly any of the missing money was recovered.

As with most rules, there were exceptions. One pal of mine, Lenny, had his house raided and, being an experienced chap, his first words were 'I want to speak to my brief.'

'Don't worry,' he was told, 'you'll be seeing him soon enough. He's in Malaga nick.'

Sure enough on arrival in Malaga the first person Lenny bumped into was his brief who had been arrested after a holdall full of cocaine was found in his car. He totally denied any knowledge of the drugs – as one would.

One afternoon, after six weeks on remand, his cell door was opened and he was told to pack his bags as he was being released. The charges had been dropped. It turned out that the National police who had 'discovered' the drugs were known to be corrupt and were under surveillance by the Guardia Civil. The Guardia actually had a video of the National police planting the drugs in the boot of the brief's car.

The brief was given profuse apologies for having had to spend six weeks in custody but it was explained to him that at the time of his arrest the Guardia weren't yet ready to proceed against the corrupt Old Bill. All this was accepted pretty philosophically by the brief who realised his career working for the defence had put a few high-ranking noses out of joint.

Back in Almeria I felt a few drinks would be right and proper and headed down to the local bar. I got talking to a Spanish girl, Maria, from Madrid who had just split up with her boyfriend and was down for a few weeks' break. We met again several times over the next week or so and we got on very well together. In fact, so well that thirty-odd years later we're still together. Maria is far from stupid but she neither asked nor was told much about my past or my then current activities, a situation that has continued to this day.

My little brush with the Old Bill hadn't put me off the puff game, far from it, the money was too good, but it did make me realise I'd have to be even more circumspect than I had been in the past. A lot of my associates in the game had the opinion that the Holy Grail of puff smuggling was getting the gear directly from Morocco but I had my doubts. The whole logistics of the job seemed beyond me and the people you had to deal with were a nightmare. In the first place you had to part with a lump of dough to some Moroccan agent who might or might not be able to do what he says he can do. Then you need a boat and a skipper. Boats don't come cheap and the sort of skippers you can find who are prepared to do the work are by and large total self-taught chancers and cowboys. If they were any good what would they need me for? Then there are the vagaries of the weather and the moon which always seem to conspire to cause another delay. On top of everything else there's the feeling of the absolute lack of any sort of control. If you pack a bit of gear in a car and there's a problem, if there's a breakdown, if the driver drops dead of a heart attack, all is not lost. Help can be rendered, cars can be repaired, and drivers can be replaced. Once the boat sets sail your fortunes are completely in the lap of the gods.

Having said all that you have to bear in mind someone has to get the gear over or we'd all be out of business and I do know a few little firms that had a remarkable degree of success. One mob in particular did very well working out of Puerto del Este in Granada. Seafaring folk refer to this place as Port Zero as it's on the Greenwich meridian

– zero degrees longitude – and it had a lot in its favour for the would-be puff smuggler. It was a sprawling place with a fair number of quite isolated berths and the adjacent town, not much more than a village, La Herradura, had little in the way of a police presence. The reason I know so much about the firm's activities is that I bought my supplies off them from time to time.

One evening I arrived to pick up a parcel only to find the three of them sitting in the lounge bar of the local hotel looking a bit glum. Fearing the worst I asked what was occurring but discovered that things weren't quite as bad as I thought. There had been a delay on the Moroccan side, not an unusual event, and they'd had to spend an extra couple of days at sea. By the time they got back their anticipated berth was occupied and they'd been allocated another which, although fairly secluded, had a major drawback. Right next to the berth was a twenty-foot floodlight tower illuminating twenty yards of quay on each side of the boat, making unloading problematical.

We had a couple of beers and mulled over the problem. After a while Herbie, the de facto boss of the outfit, said he had an idea and to give him half an hour. Sure enough, half an hour later he was back with a broad grin on his face. Apparently, using a .22 air rifle, he'd shot the bulbs out of the floodlights and the quay was now as black as a coal-mine at midnight. God almighty!! Talk about keeping a low profile, how this firm kept out of prison was a mystery.

Of course speed was now of the essence. If the boat wasn't fully unloaded that night and the bulbs were replaced the next day it would be difficult to shoot them out again without arousing grave suspicions. Off they went and after only a couple of hours' delay the gear was safely away and I was off to Almeria with my small purchase. Sometimes I feel it's better to be lucky than good.

Alfie Brown was at the top of the list when it came to professionalism but he didn't have things all his own way in the luck department. He was brilliant with fast cars and fast boats and could even fly a plane. On top of that he was as game as they come and over the years he earned fortunes. He also spent fortunes and for that reason he occasionally found himself stuck for readies. On one such occasion he put together a bit of work which was a bit lacking in his usual eye for detail. It all seemed straightforward enough – a quick dash across the Straits, pick up two hundred key, quick dash back to a secluded beach at Soto Grande and he'd earn around forty-five grand, which would solve his immediate cash shortfall.

Things went well enough on the outbound trip. The Moroccans were waiting at the appointed spot and eight twenty-five key bales were slung into the launch. It was a pitch-black night and somehow Alfie got disorientated and wound up running aground on a sandbank. For half an hour he struggled fruitlessly to free the boat but eventually he accepted that wading ashore was his only option.

With hindsight what he should have done was fire his flare-gun into the petrol tank and destroy all evidence of any skulduggery. He would then have been an unfortunate shipwrecked mariner whose boat had caught fire on impact with the sandbank. Instead of that he got on the phone to Spain to see if any assistance could be rounded up, probably thinking that it was still a bit early in the day to be writing off the boat and its cargo. The message came back to stay exactly where he was, help was on the way.

Now, as game as Alfie was, sitting on a windswept beach in Morocco a hundred yards from a boatload of puff had to be a nerve-wracking experience and he wandered off in search of some kind of shelter. A shore patrol fell across him and he was arrested. In the period between his arrest and the military going back to unload the gear a Moroccan was walking his dog along the beach and spotted the boat. He waded out and helped himself to two bales but hadn't got far before he was nicked and charged with being Alfie's accomplice. They were both sentenced to ten years and sent to the military prison in Rabat.

Alfie hadn't been in Rabat long when details of escape plans began to emerge. One scheme was to conceal some diamond-cutting wire in a tin of ham and send it to him with his regular food parcels. He was convinced that the screws, who were actually soldiers, being Muslim wouldn't open a tin of ham to check its contents. Nothing came of that plan but he soon came up with another. He began to complain of back pains and it was decided, at his own expense, to send him for treatment in the civilian hospital.

Moroccan military aren't terribly well paid and it didn't take Alfie long to pal them up, buying them coffee, Coca-Cola and giving them cigarettes. By the third hospital trip the handcuffs were dispensed with and by the fourth trip he was ready to execute his plan. Whilst one soldier was away getting the coffees in he gave the second one a shove, sending him sprawling. Running to a waiting vehicle that a couple of Scousers had left handily parked, in no time he was hurtling through the suburbs of Rabat. The Scousers were waiting a few miles away and Alfie was transferred to a van and transported to an apartment. A day or two later he travelled in a fruit lorry, concealed by several hundred sacks of dates, to Tangier.

The last part of the escape was in true James Bond style. The plan was to make the trip from Morocco to Spain by jet-ski but it was doubtful that a jet-ski would have the range. To be on the safe side two jet-skis were tied together and half way across the Straits the first one was abandoned and he continued the trip on the second one. He arrived on the beach at Algeciras to all intents and purposes a Brit tourist having a day's fun on his jet-ski. Leaving the vehicle on the beach he walked up to the main road, hailed a cab and an hour and a half later he was ensconced in a bar in Fuengirola enjoying a light ale. To this day Alfie still owes nine years, three months of his ten year sentence. No doubt the two soldiers are manning an outpost somewhere in the middle of the Sahara, the Moroccan equivalent of being sent to Siberia.

IN THE MEANTIME I was tinkering along in my own little way perfectly content with how things were going. The case I was on bail for didn't seem much to worry about. In those days, probably still so today, the law was that any case left dormant for five years became defunct. Courts had a massive backlog and any decent defence counsel worth his salt had no trouble greasing a few palms and having a file put back to the bottom of the pile until it reached its sell-by date. Strikes me as an admirable way of running a judicial system. Of course you lose your bail money but that's just part of the game.

We discovered that there was quite a number of these trucking companies running between Spain and the UK, the bulk of their cargo being made up of household effects. We rented an unfurnished apartment and made a tour of second-hand shops, buying up furniture and appliances. Fridges were particularly accommodating. Removing the insulation left plenty of room for puff without drastically affecting the weight.

Needless to say we had a few hiccups, comes with the territory, but I only recall one case of blatant underhandedness. A parcel got home and a week or so later one of the buyers slightly lower down the food chain returned twenty key saying it was crap. A quick look by our people at the stamps on the bars established that it wasn't the gear we had sent. There followed a few days of one of those oh-yes-it-is oh-no-it-isn't arguments but when the buyers realised who they were dealing with they admitted that perhaps a mistake had been made. A courier came over with the forty grand. Other than that the only problems were the odd parcel getting captured, but again that comes with the territory.

I've always been an ambitious type of person and when things are going well it's difficult not to start thinking bigger, but those large scale operations had a wealth of inherent dangers. The more people involved the bigger risk of a leak. Then there's the logistics of loading a wagon what with warehouses, fork-lifts and pallets and the same again at the other end getting it off. And the driver. If you pay a driver fifty grand to take a few hundred key home there's a major risk that his nervousness at the customs will give the game away. Our drivers, not knowing there was any contraband aboard, had no reason to be nervous. And the money. If a driver who has been struggling through on his hundred and fifty quid a week suddenly falls into fifty grand, what's he going to do with it? Well, I'll tell you what he's going to do. First he'll want a nice new car. Then he'll be down the local betting shop having oners or twoers on horses where he used to have three fifty pence doubles and a fifty pence treble. He'll be in the boozer making a Big Time Charlie Potatoes of himself buying rounds for all his pals. Before long all his neighbours will be speculating from whence his new found affluence has come, the Old Bill will get wind, surveillance will be mounted and in no time everyone will finish up in the nick. I vowed to resist the urge for expansion.

Needless to say my presence in Mojacar hadn't gone unnoticed by the local Old Bill. There was one particular sergeant, Paco, that was the bane of all the expats' lives. Tourists were accepted as pretty much a necessary evil but the expats were looked on a little differently. Quite understandable really I suppose. Here was this sergeant rubbing along on his pittance a week and seeing us do little else but lie in the sun and have a drink. He'd make it his business to accost us at any opportunity.

Things changed a little at the time of Charlie's murder. He came over to me in a bar that night offering his condolences and asking me if I knew anything about what had gone on. I told him, quite truthfully, that I had no idea and I'd only heard that it was done by a paid hit man. We never got to the stage of becoming chatty-chatty but we did develop more of a live-and-let-live relationship.

One night, for reasons best known to themselves, the Old Bill decided to give me a spin and Paco was in charge of the rummage team. Apart from one tiny piece of personal puff nothing untoward was found. Paco told the underlings to ignore it and was only too pleased to give a written report that everything was hunky-dory.

Another complication came with the passing years. Having sourced your bit of gear, got it home, got it sold and got the money back over, what did you actually do with the money? Other than spend it, not much. The good old days when, by walking into a bank with a passport and a sack of money, you'd already answered all the questions you were ever likely to be asked were long gone. Depositing cash into an account was getting more and more difficult and anything over about three grand impossible. Cheques left a trail and money laundering became a catch-all charge for anyone that was suspected but couldn't be nicked for puff smuggling.

When buying property it had been standard procedure to walk into a notary's office with a small cheque and a large envelope of readies. That stopped happening and property had to change hands on paper at close to its real value.

Even second-hand car dealers, not generally regarded as the world's most scrupulous traders, were reluctant to take cash. If they did they were faced with the same problem of getting the money into an account. Jewellery and other luxury items were much the same story.

This might all sound like not a bad problem to have but it was another disincentive to play any bigger than your expenditure required.

Spending money in bars, restaurants and clothes shops in Spain wasn't frowned upon like it was in the UK Expats were expected, practically obliged, to spend money like drunken sailors and I did treat myself to a few luxuries without raising too many eyebrows. Probably that's why, despite a very reasonable income, I wasn't making any significant headway in accumulating a vast amount of money. This was no great worry because, like everyone else in the game, I assumed it would all go on forever. Of course we were wrong. Once it was realised the kind of money involved more and more people jumped in, who could blame them, and the loads got bigger and bigger. The inevitable result was that the price in the UK began to go through the floor.

In the early eighties fifty key was considered a respectable sized parcel but by the early nineties a ton was looked on as being a bit on the shabby side. The days of gear making two grand a key at the top end of the wholesale market were gone forever. By the turn of the millennium anyone could go out on the streets of London or Manchester and buy a single key for less than a grand. Granted the prices had gone down in Spain as well but the whole risk-to-gain ratio had gone out the window. Perhaps we should have gone at it hammer and tongs when the game was good.

When things were flying Maria and I bought a very nice four-bedroomed walled villa complete with a pool, barbecue and the other trimmings paying a very reasonable price for it. The flat we rented out to a friend. When things began to go downhill we sold the villa and moved back to the flat. Eventually, inland, we found a very rustic small-holding with plenty of land that suited us perfectly and bought it for less than it was worth. We've lived there very happily for the last twelve years.

I hadn't been in the new place long when we had one of those horrendous storms they get over here, hailstones, thunder and lightning, the lot. The weather is marvellous ninety-odd per cent of the time but when they have a bit of rain they don't mess about. The nearest neighbour, a carpenter, lived a couple of hundred yards away and he came out to his porch to use his mobile phone. Next thing there's a massive bang and a flash and the poor fella disappeared in a ball of smoke. Struck by lightning. Some people have no luck.

Most people think that Spaghetti Westerns were made in Italy but they weren't, they were mainly made in Almeria. The Italian connection was that Sergio Leone directed the bulk of the genre. Some of the studios have survived to this day and two or three have become mini theme parks.

Mini Hollywood is the set used for the Clint Eastwood trilogy *A Fistful of Dollars*, *For a Few Dollars More* and *The Good, The Bad and The Ugly*. The place was built in 1966 by Sergio Leone's designer, Carlo Simi, and to this day you can see the El Paso bank robbed in the film or even have a light ale in the saloon. Maybe run into the ghost of Lee Van Cleef. North of Almeria town on the Granada road is 'Ranch Leone' where Leone filmed *Once Upon A Time in the West* with Henry Fonda and Charles Bronson. The ruins of 'Flagstone' can still be seen. Carboneras is a little more upmarket. This was the setting for the epic *Lawrence of Arabia* with Peter O'Toole and Omar Sharif.

After the Spaghetti Western boom had run its course and before the theme parks came into being the sets were used by a British company making TV commercials. A lot of impoverished locals and expats got work as extras on these shoots. There was a series of ads for British Telecom with the slogan 'It's For You'. One ad showed General Custer surrounded by Sitting Bull and his mob when the phone rings.

'What's that you say? Reinforcements are on the way?'

Sitting Bull shrugs his shoulders and they begin to wander off.

'Oh, okay. They'll be here tomorrow,' says Custer.

The Indians cheer and go and bash up Custer and his men.

One scene required a volunteer to be suspended by his ankles from an arched gateway. A pal, Micky Reilly, stepped forward. They didn't bother with cissy stuff like body harnesses or anything, relying on a couple of strapping fellows to lend support until the take was made. By take fifteen Mick was about an inch and a half taller than he had been before take one. He was in agony for months.

Another series of ads was for American Express with the slogan 'That'll Do Nicely, Sir'. A horde of Viking marauders land on a deserted beach but instead of raping and pillaging they produce Am-Ex cards. 'That'll do nicely, sir,' says the head man of the invaded Saxon village. A pal of mine, Stan the Man, got a small part which I thought was very ironic since he had just finished serving a prison sentence – for credit card fraud!

Apart from the film studios there was very little in the way of local industry. The terrain was very arid and full of ravines, not too suitable for agriculture. Then someone came up with a scheme to grow fruit and vegetables under polythene sheeting which meant farmers could produce four or five crops a year instead of one. Nowadays you can drive for miles and see nothing but polythene hangars and the area has some of the richest farmers in Spain.

On 28 February 2013, I heard the news Bruce had died. It came as quite a shock because to the best of my knowledge he'd been in reasonably good health for an eighty-one-year old. Thankfully he died peacefully in his sleep. Knowing Bruce and I had been very close, Tommy Wisbey phoned me to offer his condolences and during the conversation he told me Jimmy White had also left us. Jimmy was probably the least high profile of all of us and I hadn't heard much of him over the years so his death was news to me. All this was only months after Jimmy Hussey had passed away.

Shortly after Bruce came home from prison he spent a couple of weeks with me at my flat in Mojacar. On the last night we sat on the balcony drinking whiskey until the sun came up. Living all his life in central London, and with all the years spent in prison, Bruce hadn't had the opportunity to experience those spectacular sunrises you often get in southern Spain. He turned to me and said, 'You know, Gordon, now I think you've found what you were always looking for.'

By coincidence that part of town is known as the Corner of Enchantment and I thought it was an appropriate spot to sit and raise a glass to my old pal on the day of his funeral.

Ill-health had prevented me attending in person but my daughter went and read a short message from me. She phoned me during the afternoon and said someone wanted to speak to me.

'You owe me a few quid,' said an unfamiliar voice.

'Who are you?' I asked.

'Don't you know? You sold me a bike in 1943 and it turned out to be stolen. I finished up getting nicked and fined two quid. My dad went mad. Where can I pick up my two quid?'

I couldn't place the bloke but then I probably sold numerous stolen bikes back then. We did a bit of reminiscing during which I learned he was from around the corner from me in Fulham. He remembered the bombing in Putney Bridge Road as vividly as I did.

Freddie Foreman also rang from the funeral and sounded in fine fettle despite having turned eighty a fortnight earlier.

One annoying detail of the funeral was that all the news reports, reinforcing my aversion to the paparazzi, seemed to start along the lines 'Ronnie Biggs attends Bruce Reynolds's funeral.' Whilst it may be true that Biggsy became the best known of the train robbers because of his escape and his time on the run, it's equally true that he was the least important. He came onto the work at the last moment and then only because he was a friend of Bruce's and because he led us to believe he had a man who could move the train. All his exploits whilst on the run did none of us any favours in the eyes of the parole board.

SOMETIMES I FEEL more Spanish than English, having spent more time here than anywhere else. I can't begin to tell you how much I've enjoyed my years living in Spain. The weather, the people, the lifestyle, the food and drink. Without a doubt my decision to move here was the best choice I ever made in my life. Of late I've not been in the best of health but the treatment I've been provided with by the National Health Service couldn't be bettered in Harley Street.

Unlike many of my fellow Costa del Sol residents I'm perfectly free to travel back to the UK In the early days I did make numerous trips back but as the years went by I began to find fewer and fewer reasons to go. I doubt very much if I'll ever set foot in the place again.

One time I was in the departure lounge at Heathrow awaiting a flight back to Malaga when the old 'cozzer red alert' switched itself on. I'd spotted a bloke at the bar who kept staring at me so I wandered over to the book stall to keep an eye on him whilst apparently browsing. He was soon joined by a woman and there was no doubt from the covert looks and muttered conversation they were talking about me. The flight was called and I was no sooner seated than the couple boarded and took a couple of seats in the row in front of me.

Waiting to collect my luggage at Malaga I turned around and saw the couple heading straight for me. I was racking my brains to think of what bit of nonsense I might have been up to that had led to me getting a look at but nothing came to mind.

'Señor Gordon?' the man said.

I suddenly realised that I knew the man but was stumped as to how. Then it came to me. In the early sixties, one of my favourite watering holes was Antonio's Restaurant in Long Acre, Soho. They had a great Spanish menu and a wonderful atmosphere and I used it frequently. Although I hadn't seen him for forty years I recognised him as the wine waiter from Antonio's and his companion was his wife, Dolores, the flamenco singer from the place. It turned out they were off to Cadiz to visit Dolores's mother. We were all delighted to meet up again after all those years even if he had almost given me a heart attack thinking it was on me.

Another blast from the past came about by a chance encounter in a bar in Mojacar. I got talking to a retired couple who had recently moved over from England.

'Whereabouts in London did you live?' I asked at one point.

'Putney,' the man said.

'Oh, yeah? That was my manor. Whereabouts in Putney?'

'We lived on the Upper Richmond Road,' he said.

'I know the Upper Richmond Road well,' I said. 'What part did you live on?'

'Halfway down. We had a flat above a greengrocer's shop.

Well, fuck me, what a small world. They'd only moved into the greengrocer's flat that I'd screwed in 1960 and made off with the eleven grand in biscuit tins. I remembered it so well I was even able to describe their old bedroom to them. We still laugh about it to this day.

These days Maria and I live a very quiet life on the smallholding in the hills above Mojacar. We keep six dogs and three cats and did keep a few chickens until Maria put her foot down. I still enjoy a glass of wine and even the occasional Jameson's and Maria being a great cook, we eat well. At my age what more could I ask?

One pastime I get a lot of pleasure from these days is sitting in my garden and watching the myriad birds swoop in and out of the trees. There's a pair of kestrels nesting in one of my trees and a family of bee-catchers in another. These bee-catchers are the most colourful birds I've ever seen, with their plumage of half a dozen or more shades of blue, green, red and yellow. They dart about all day catching and swallowing all kinds of insects in mid-air. I often sit and watch them for hours and I know I've really been blessed to have found this place.

Whilst admittedly my life has had its ups and downs, it has been a very adventurous one and there's really not a lot I would change. Well, there is one thing. If I had it all to do again I'd make damn sure that the farm was burnt down!

The Jail Birds

THIS YEAR WORMWOOD Scrubs prison – an establishment renowned for its more eminent residents – was graced with the presence of two more unusual 'jail birds' who have not only brought a breath of life to the everyday routine but also created history within the prison environs.

So far as can be ascertained birds of prey have never been seen here, but this summer two kestrels have nested in a disused turret of the south wing of 'D' Hall. Unfortunately adequate observation cannot be made on the grounds of security. Representations made to the governor have not proved successful, although hopes for the future are harboured should the pair return to mate next season. Meanwhile all attempts at observation have to be made from ground level and at irregular times each day; thus details of the birds' activities, number of eggs, exact location, etc., etc. are sparse.

The male has frequently been seen getting off in search of food and returning with some type of rodent in its talons. Once three or four inmates were treated to the exciting spectacle of seeing the male chase and capture a sparrow near the perimeter fence.

The female is not seen as often as the male which leads us to assume she is busy creating her 'nest eggs'. Naturally we cannot tell whether the birds have been ringed but if they return it is hoped that interest can be generated among members of The Bird Society, whose activities are normally confined to the breeding of cage birds, and pressure under their aegis can be brought upon authorities to allow a more competent and systematic method of observation. Meanwhile we can only watch from afar and share the pleasure of their company, comforted with the knowledge that even such an awe-inspiring edifice as a prison is capable of providing a home for two creatures all too often misunderstood and needlessly abused.

Gordon Goody
Wormwood Scrubs
1973